Warrior · 48

English Medieval Knight 1200–1300

Christopher Gravett · Illustrated by Graham Turner

First published in Great Britain in 2002 by Osprey Publishing, Elms Court, Chapel Way, Botley, Oxford OX2 9LP, United Kingdom.
Email: info@ospreypublishing.com

ISBN 1 84176 144 3

Editor: Marcus Cowper
Design: Ken Vail Graphic Design, Cambridge, UK
Index by Susan Williams
Originated by Grasmere Digital Imaging, Leeds, UK
Printed in China through World Print Ltd.

02 03 04 05 06   10 9 8 7 6 5 4 3 2 1

FOR A CATALOGUE OF ALL BOOKS PUBLISHED BY OSPREY MILITARY AND AVIATION PLEASE CONTACT:

The Marketing Manager, Osprey Direct USA,
c/o Motorbooks International, PO Box 1,
Osceola, WI 54020-0001, USA.
Email: info@ospreydirectusa.com

The Marketing Manager, Osprey Direct UK, PO Box 140,
Wellingborough, Northants, NN8 4ZA, United Kingdom.
Email: info@ospreydirect.co.uk

www.ospreypublishing.com

Artist's note

Readers may care to note that the original paintings from which the colour plates in this book were prepared are available for private sale. All reproduction copyright whatsoever is retained by the Publishers. All enquiries should be addressed to:

Graham Turner,
PO Box 88,
Chesham,
Buckinghamshire
HP5 2SR
UK

The Publishers regret that they can enter into no correspondence upon this matter.

FRONT COVER **A scene from the *Trinity Apocalypse* of *c*.1250–60. (Reproduced by permission of the Master and Fellows of Trinity College Cambridge, MS R.16.2, f.23r)**

CONTENTS

ENGLISH MEDIEVAL KNIGHT 1200-1300

INTRODUCTION

The 13th century was a time of change for knights in England. They were faced with rising costs and increasing demands on their time for local government because of their very status in society, until knighthood itself was sometimes avoided. Feudal service would be increasingly supplemented by pay especially for duty beyond the borders of England.

Since 1199 England had been ruled by John. His co-ordinated plan to raise the siege of Château Gaillard in 1203 went wrong, and Normandy was lost to Philip II of France the following year. There was still an English presence in Gascony, but John's efforts to assist the German Emperor, Otto IV, against Philip II of France failed and the Emperor's forces were beaten at Bouvines in 1214. This was the final straw as far as some barons were concerned, and led to Magna Carta the following year. John repudiated the charter as soon as he felt able and civil war soon broke out, continuing after his death in 1216 during the minority of his son, Henry III. Prince Louis of France and his allies besieged Dover and Lincoln but were foiled and withdrew.

In 1227 Henry declared himself fit to govern, but not until 1232 did he feel strong enough to challenge the rule of Hubert de Burgh, his justiciar or chief minister. A king who was happiest with the arts, his expeditions against Llywelyn ap Iorweth of Wales failed miserably and he vainly campaigned in France to seize lost territories. He upset many barons by his demands for various taxes, known as aids and scutages, by the extortion allowed the sheriffs, and by royal generosity to foreigners such as his own Poitevin half-brothers, the Lusignans, William and Aymer de Valence, bishop elect of Winchester. Richard Marshal, whom Henry eventually disgraced, in alliance with Llywelyn carried on a civil war against the Poitevins.

In 1254 Henry accepted the crown of Sicily for his son, Edmund, as the Pope strove to break the power of the Hohenstaufen German emperors there. Expected to send English troops, Henry faced baronial opposition though a German victory made further moves more unlikely. Three years later Henry's brother, Richard, Earl of Cornwall, was elected King of the Romans (the title for the heir to the Holy Roman Empire), a hope that never materialised. Baronial discontent came to a head in the Parliament of London, in 1258; a rising force, 'the community of the bachelry of England', came increasingly to prominence. Their leader was Simon de Montfort, Earl of Leicester, son of a noted Albigensian crusader and Henry's brother-in-law. A number of magnates were jealous of this Gascon who now virtually ruled England and once again civil war erupted, known as the Barons' War. Henry, freed from the

French war by the Peace of Paris in 1259, now challenged Simon. At the battle at Lewes (1264) Henry was himself captured but Simon's government was short lived, and he was killed at Evesham the following year. In 1266 the siege of Kenilworth ended the campaign.

When Henry died in 1272 he left the crown to his able son, the tall and warlike Edward I. Prince Edward had led a small English contingent to the Holy Land before his coronation, and English knights were present in other crusading bodies. He is perhaps best known as the 'Hammer of the Scots', but it was the Welsh who first encountered him when Prince Llywelyn ap Gruffydd refused homage in 1272. Edward seized the corn supplies in Anglesey with a fleet and forced the prince, trapped in Snowdonia, to surrender in 1277. He rebelled again in 1282, prompting a full invasion and Llywelyn's death in a skirmish. Edward was a prolific castle builder and a serious Welsh uprising in 1294, the same year that war with France broke out over Gascony, saw Edward's castles prove their worth. In 1297 he took a large army across to Flanders to block the expansion of Philip IV but was hampered partly by recalcitrance at the huge scale of military aid he tried to enlist, and a truce was arranged. With John Balliol's revolt in 1296 the Scottish Wars of Independence began. Despite a setback with William Wallace's success at Stirling Bridge in 1297, the now ageing King Edward won

A wall painting from All Saints Church, Claverley, Shropshire, probably executed around the turn of the 13th century and probably depicting the battle between vices and virtues. The knights, some in surcoats, wear flat-topped, round or conical helmets, with rather crudely painted face-masks.

victory at Falkirk in 1298, but the wars would drag on beyond the king's death in 1307.

CHRONOLOGY

1199	Death of Richard I. Accession of John.
1203–4	Siege of Château Gaillard by Philip II.
1204	Loss of Normandy.
1214	Battle of Bouvines.
1215	Magna Carta. Siege of Rochester castle.
1216	Death of John. Minority of Henry III. Siege of Dover castle by Prince Louis.
1217	Second battle of Lincoln.
1224	Siege of Bedford castle.
1227	Henry III assumes reins of government.
1258	Barons' Parliament.
1259	Peace of Paris with France.
1264	Battle of Lewes.
1265	Battle of Evesham. Death of Simon de Montfort
1266	Siege of Kenilworth castle.
1272	Death of Henry III. Accession of Edward I.
1277	First Welsh War.
1282	Second Welsh War.
1296	First Scottish campaign. Scotland annexed to England.
1297	Flanders campaign. Truce with Philip IV of France
1297	Battle of Stirling Bridge.

A copper-alloy moulded mace-head, probably of late 12th or early 13th-century date. (By courtesy of the Trustees of the Armouries, VIII.250)

1298	Second Scottish campaign. Battle of Falkirk.
1300	Third Scottish campaign. Siege of Caerlaverock castle.
1301	Fourth Scottish campaign.
1303–4	Fifth Scottish campaign.
1305	Execution of William Wallace.
1307	Death of Edward I. Accession of Edward II.

ORGANISATION

The forces of English kings and magnates in the 13th century were made up from several elements. Household 'knights' formed the core of fighting men, a group made up of bannerets, knights and squires directly serving their lord or king, whose numbers could be augmented by several means. The old idea of military service as a feudal obligation, though still alive, was diminishing in importance, increasingly being supplemented or replaced by service in return for pay. The idea of using wages was not new, but the extent to which this method would be employed, and the idea of military contracts that also developed, was different. In contrast to this new type of military–financial arrangement we also still find magnates who followed the king for nothing but honour and sometimes a desire to avenge themselves on their enemies.

There were several ways a knight could join a retinue, the usual avenues being as a family member, as a household knight, or as a military tenant. Kinsmen provided an obvious source of warriors for a lord. In 1297, for the Flanders and Falkirk campaigns, Aymer de Valence contracted with Thomas and Maurice Berkeley for knights and troopers for a fixed fee in peace, to serve at the usual wages in war, themselves serving as bannerets with two squires each, the knights with one each besides troopers.

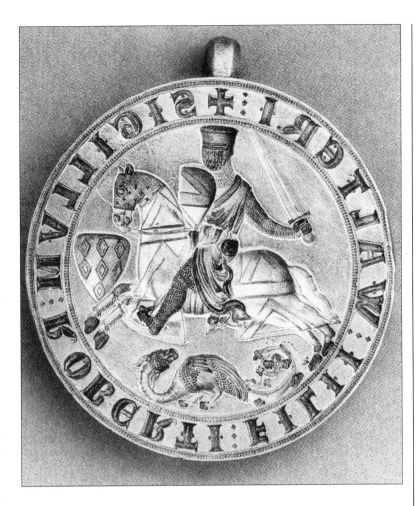

The early 13th-century silver seal die of Robert FitzWalter, showing what appears to be a padded testier on the horse's head and neck. (Reproduced by courtesy of the Trustees of the British Museum, Dept of Medieval and Modern Europe, 1841, 6–24, 1)

The familia

Harking back to the Germanic hearth troop, lords had their *familia* ('family') of paid household knights. This provided fighting men at short notice and was especially valuable in conquered or turbulent regions such as the marches on the borders with Wales or Scotland. The knights and squires who composed a *familia* might become close to their lord. When near death in 1219, for example, William Marshal refused to allow the sale of his furs and robes to raise money for alms, since he wanted them to go to his household knights.

One of a pair of early 13th-century prick spurs, with slotted arms for the leathers. (By courtesy of the Trustees of the Armouries, VI.331)

The king's *familia* similarly made up the nucleus of the royal army, with as many soldiers as the feudal contingents, and this important body grew in size. The bannerets, knights bachelor and troopers in the royal *familia* drew rations and pay (4 shillings a banneret and 2 shillings a knight) but when on active service the knights received 3 shillings, perhaps to pay for extra rations or to pay the orderly who accompanied them. The household knights did a variety of jobs, ferrying prisoners, bringing up infantry or workmen, overseeing castles, or helping to govern conquered areas. Some stayed close to the king. Henry III had 30 or more knights receiving fees from the exchequer, while others seem to have been summoned. A muster list for the military household from 1225–6 reveals a total force of 97 knights (about 200 when their own retainers were added). Pay accounts mention that 527 out of 895 men bound for the Flanders campaign of 1297 were members of the household. Gascons and Spaniards were included in the royal *familia.*

Household knights and retinues varied in number, but Henry could probably raise 100 or more knights quickly. Such figures varied depending on royal requirements and money, and generally fell between 40 and 80 knights and bannerets. To this figure must be added squires and sergeants of the household, some 170 in about 1285, plus the retinues of the knights themselves. Each knight had to keep two squires and three horses. The king provided horses and sometimes gave armours or pieces of armour

Permanent units of mercenary knights and crossbowmen were also attached to the royal forces. John employed large numbers under such men as Fawkes de Bréauté, honourably mentioned at the second battle of Lincoln in 1217. Magna Carta attempted to expel all foreign mercenaries from the country and numbers diminished after this, but in 1230 Henry III may have hired as many as 500 knights and 1,000 sergeants in Poitou. In 1242 some 700 mercenary crossbowmen were in the English army campaigning in France and Edward I hired 1,523 crossbowmen from Gascony in 1282, compared to 173 household knights and bannerets and 72 squires. Mercenaries were usually arranged in constabularies of 100 men, the individual troops composing these averaging 10 to 15 men, and 25 to 35 for the commander of the unit. The usual period of paid service was 40 days at a time, reflecting feudal duty.

At Falkirk in 1298 the total strength of the household troops plus associated mercenaries was slightly less than 800 men, compared to only 564 supplied by the nobles. In 1300 the household cavalry and mercenaries came to 522, as opposed to 40 knights and 366 sergeants from the feudal summons. From 1277 Welsh footsoldiers were recruited into the royal forces.

The feudal system

Feudal society had come to England with William the Conqueror in 1066. Magnates received land, often scattered over a number of areas, in

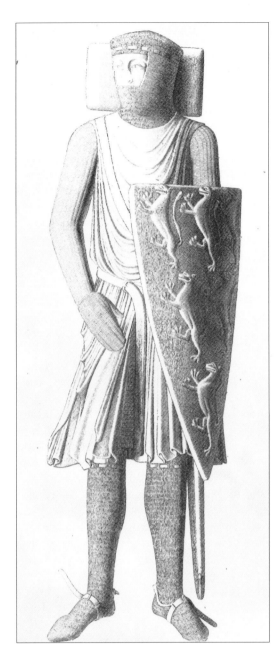

The effigy of William Longespée in Salisbury Cathedral, dated around 1230–40, is the earliest surviving English military effigy, though restored in the 19th century. Note the lace threaded through the mail links to keep the coif in place; the shape of the latter suggests a padded arming cap beneath designed for a helm. The square end of the laced ventail is also visible, as are the laces threaded through the mail below the knees.

return for military service. Lesser lords might in turn be enfeoffed of the magnates, though some held directly from the king. Some knights held land from several lords, in which case the most powerful usually became their liege lord, the one they followed above all others excepting the king himself. Such sub-infeudation weakened a lord's hold on his men, and could lead to court cases. Homage was a formal ceremony in front of witnesses when the man knelt before his prospective lord and placed his hands between those of the latter, then swore to be his man and to follow him. The oath of fealty was also taken. The new vassal, or tenant, was then given some token to signify the agreement, such as a glove or flag. By the 13th century the knight's fee was assessed on property rather than on land held, so that men could be summoned who could afford the costs involved.

Tenure by knight service

Initially magnates were expected to serve in person with their full agreed quota of knights, this included two or more troopers in each knight's retinue. Lesser barons could make up their quota of knights using the notion that one knight was worth two retainers; thus a requirement of six might be made up of three knights and six retainers. Unlike the richer bannerets, many knights brought perhaps a single squire and one or two other followers. A few tenants-in-chief did feudal service under an earl rather than bring several horsemen to the larger muster. Service required beyond 40 days was usually paid, though some, out of pride or hatred for the enemy, refused to take payment.

As soon as scutage ('shield money': a tax paid by knights in lieu of performing military service) was accepted in the 12th century, knight's fees could be held by people with no intention of becoming knights. By the early 13th century some 80 per cent of the 5,000 knights in the country paid scutage or fines, rather than serve in person. At this time the feudal knights of William Marshal composed only about one third of his men, though other evidence shows a lord's retinue could often be composed largely of his tenants. Records surviving from Edward I's reign show that many magnates rarely served in person. After the first Welsh war in 1277 sheriffs were ordered to collect scutage at 40 shillings per knight's fee.

Feudal troops serving their tenant-in-chief seem to have been paid, but when serving to fulfil the tenant's obligation to the king, the service was at their own expense. Sometimes the service was performed without a summons being issued, and by the end of the century this type of service was often performed for pay.

Some men saw the opportunity of obtaining land or privileges by offering the king knight service. John was in need of men for his

Detail from the Longespée effigy
showing the edge of the ventail
and laces.

projected French campaign in 1205, and was especially likely to respond at this time. In that year he ordered that all knights in every shire should be constrained by the sheriffs to send one from every ten knights of the shire to the royal host, to be armed and paid by the other nine at a rate of 2 shillings a day. It seems the king expected these knights to stay with him as long as he needed them, and no length of service was specified. The army was gathered but did not cross the Channel.

On occasion two knights came to a mutual agreement called brotherhood in arms. A brotherhood agreement from 1298 is a rare survivor of a common practice, by which gains were shared as well as losses, and the two knights mutually supported one another.

As well as military service in the field, knights were expected to perform castle-guard at the tenant-in-chief's castle or a local royal fortress. Service varied, from 15 days a year to four months in every twelve. Some knights were expected to do the service only in wartime; some were exempted from service in the army, others had to do both. By the 13th century castle-guard service was commonly commuted for money to pay for mercenaries. Marcher lords held strongholds along the borders with Wales, which they helped to subjugate. Marcher lords on the Scottish borders were constantly called out to repel raids.

A time of change

At the beginning of the 13th century the nature of feudal service began to change. The system that had been in use for several centuries could not supply the requirements of a modern fighting force. One pressing problem was the need for men to fight in long campaigns outside England, something for which the traditional 40-day feudal service limit was not well designed. Another was the rising cost of knighthood, of equipping horsemen. Paying knights at 2 shillings per man per day meant that it would be extremely expensive for a magnate to provide as many fully armoured cavalry as had been expected in the previous century, when prices were much lower. New royal feudal bargains reflected this, with much lower demands for men. Some magnates simply did not bring their full quotas when summoned. In 1214 the Earl of Devon brought 20 knights, rather than the 89 he actually owed. According to the Unknown Charter, issued before Magna Carta, the barons believed that anyone owing over ten knights should have their service reduced. As

well as magnates and their large retinues, John summoned individual knights from great honours such as Tickhill, who often came alone or with one knight. Unusually, John gave repayable prests (cash advances) to those performing feudal service, as in the Irish expedition of 1210 and that in Poitou in 1214.

Magna Carta did not reduce quotas, only prevented further burdens. Individual bargains, however, did result in a large decrease in the size of the feudal call-up for magnates, though lesser lords did not feel anything like so great a benefit. The occasional inclusion of countesses in the lists indicates that personal service was not demanded, however. In 1229 about 500–600 knights were collected. Courtenay had owed 92 knights but now only had to provide three; Robert of St John sent five instead of 55, and actually owed only three. Robert of Newborough's quota had been reduced from 15 to 12 but he still only supplied two knights. Nor were knights' fees greatly enlarged to go with the reduced quotas. Magnates who had owed large numbers of men would have incurred huge expenses to bring them all, and a large number in reserve ensured a supply for a long campaign. It was perhaps also safer for the crown that such

Though not part of the English military scene, this amusing rendition of a war elephant does include soldiers. In this illustration of c.1230–40, the flat-topped helm with deep face-plate is even worn by a crossbowman. Some shorter-sleeved mail coats and kettle hats are in use. Note the axes and sling, whose lead or stone missiles were lethal when they struck an unprotected head. (By permission of the British Library, MS Harley 4751, f.8)

lords did not get into the habit of raising impressive forces, which could be dangerous. In 1282 the Earls of Norfolk and Hereford withdrew with their quotas after their 40-day service, highlighting the dangerous gap that would have been left had their whole retinues been present.

These new quotas were too small to be practical, and it is significant that the crown (and lords in their turn) still demanded scutage at the old rate. Fines were levied for underpayment of scutage or refusal to send adequate numbers of men, but there were many occasions when the fines were carried over and large sums remained owing. In 1263 the tenants-in-chief were mustered with these new quotas, but the sheriffs were also charged to muster all those holding at least a knight's fee. Feudal service was thus still used to summon men, complete with references to fealty and homage, or in some cases one or the other. The Barons' Wars of the mid-century were still feudal in character.

Churchmen whose landholdings made them liable to military duties usually contracted with a professional to provide the necessary men for feudal service.

Although it might have been simpler for the kings to move to an entirely money-based military system, objections from the nobles to their feudal duties being replaced by wages caused the continuation of the summons. When Edward I tried to raise troops for Gascony in 1294 the muster had to be postponed because of poor attendance. However, campaigns such as Flanders (1297) and Falkirk (1298) were conducted without a feudal summons.

Paid service

By Edward I's reign greater finances were available especially from taxation, customs duties and credit obtained from Italian merchants. Edward was thus able to recruit much larger armies than previously, and paid troops were useful in campaigns such as those in Wales and Scotland. In 1277 and 1282 some retainers were taken into pay after their 40-day feudal service, for periods of 40 days at a time. In 1282 Edward offered pay to six earls and many tenants-in-chief but six weeks later there was a full feudal levy. Many magnates, perhaps not wishing to be equated with mercenaries, served voluntarily and did not accept royal pay. However, such voluntary service could not go on indefinitely, and almost all barons

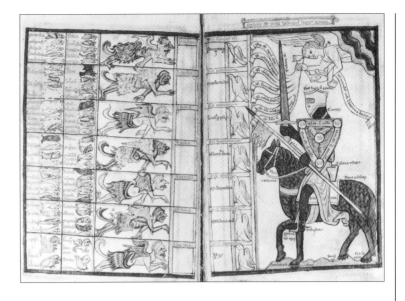

ABOVE 'The just man', a virtuous mounted English knight facing evils, from the *Summa de Vitiis* of Peraldus, made *c.*1240. (By permission of the British Library, MS Harley 3244, ff.27v–28r)

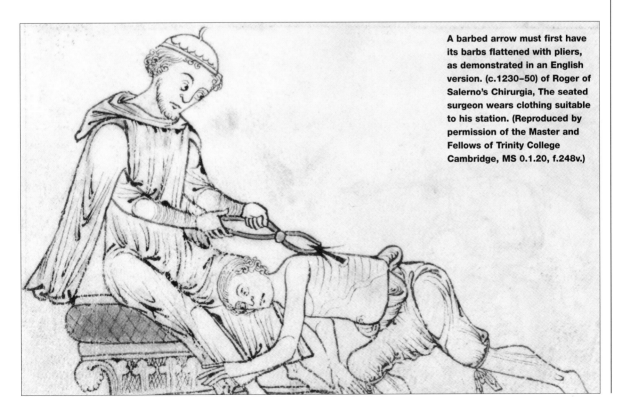

A barbed arrow must first have its barbs flattened with pliers, as demonstrated in an English version. (c.1230–50) of Roger of Salerno's Chirurgia, The seated surgeon wears clothing suitable to his station. (Reproduced by permission of the Master and Fellows of Trinity College Cambridge, MS 0.1.20, f.248v.)

served for pay at some time. The first surviving contract for pay dates in 1270; the king first used them in the 1290s for campaigning in Gascony. In 1294 writs were served to 54 tenants-in-chief for paid duty in Gascony. For an expedition such as that of 1298 – the largest force raised by contract in Edward's reign – the paid troops appear to have composed between a quarter and a third of the forces. Horsemen in the king's pay were provided with their own arms, armour and horses. The king often gave favourite bannerets valuable animals, as well as armours or pieces of armour and horses lost in service were replaced. A document of 1283 directed that arms and armour lost in royal service in war were to be made good, and mentions 200 shields, 140 headless lances and 120 lance-heads. In the unpaid feudal host such losses fell to the baron or retainer.

The horse valuation lists provide a figure of about 1,300 men receiving pay at this time, which Michael Prestwich suggests gives a total figure of perhaps 4,000 knights, squires and sergeants. The Earl of Surrey had six squadrons in pay, a total of 500 horse, and could raise another 200. Roger Bigod, Earl of Norfolk, commanded five bannerets, nine knights and 17 men-at-arms. Financial accounts do not take note of non-combatants such as grooms or valets. However, the majority of cavalry were probably not generally in receipt of wages from the king.

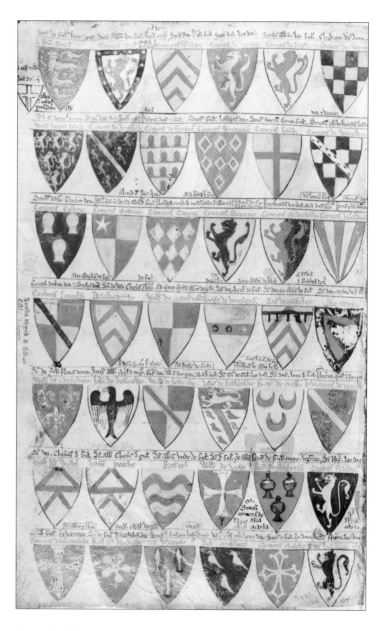

The earliest known roll of arms. A sheet of 42 coats-of-arms, by Matthew Paris, painted c.1244. The royal arms are shown at top left. There are another 33 shields on the reverse side. (By permission of the British Library, MS Cotton Nero D I, f.171v)

By late century there was a rapid turnover of membership of retinues, men serving a different lord on each campaign, and personal loyalty was rare, one exception being Robert Clifford. Many knights came with only one or two followers, and were paid independently. It is uncertain whether they were placed in informal groups or perhaps, more likely, were given some independence within larger divisions. In the 1300 campaign John de St John had 65 followers, by far the largest single group, but there were many small ones.

Composition of troops

The captain of a paid squadron was normally of rank. Bannerets were usually tenants-in-chief but often with small feudal obligations, with perhaps 13 to 15 followers; some were themselves part of a large retinue.

Bannerets could also be promoted from knights-bachelor, a change signified by cutting the end off the knightly pennon to make the square or rectangular banner. These were often landowners living near to each other and their captain. Even when tenants-in-chief were present, it was rare for them actually to serve in person, most instead using a substitute.

In the early 13th century knights, squires and sergeants appear roughly equal on pay rolls. By the time of Edward I the squire received the same as the mounted sergeant. In the Welsh wars, squires riding armoured horses were paid 1 shilling per day, but those on unprotected horses received only 6d or 8d. Military pay records show that, under Edward I, between a quarter and a third of cavalry were knights, the rest being squires, sergeants and other men-at-arms. In the second Welsh war of 1282–83, of those mustered at Chester, 28 per cent were knights or bannerets, while at Gloucester it was 24 per cent.

Hobilars were light cavalry of Irish origin first used in Scotland in 1296; other types of light-armed horsemen had been in use on the Welsh march for over a century.

In the early part of the century, knights often out-numbered sergeants, but the ratio was changing. For the Welsh war of 1277, 228 knights and 294 sergeants served for 40 days without pay, with two sergeants equated to one knight in discharging their obligations. Only 40 knights were on the Caerlaverock campaign in 1300, but the number of sergeants had increased to 366. By this date sergeant (*serviens*) was the rank below a knight, as was squire (*scutifer*) and valet (*valletti*), which appears to be another term for squire (as was *armiger*).

During the 13th century the organisation of cavalry units seems to have undergone a change. At the beginning of the century they were usually divided into units or multiples of ten, called **conrois**, as had been used in Norman England. A unit of ten men seems to make up the **constabularia**.

A document from late in Edward's reign suggests royal household cavalry were still organised into *constabularia*. Most cavalry by this time, however, was divided into the retinues of bannerets and

A praying crusader, drawn by Matthew Paris in about 1250. The unarmoured palms, and the ventail pulled across and tied at the temple, are clearly visible. The small crosses rising from his shoulders may be attached to some form of cuirie, or an upper chest and throat defence, perhaps an explanation for some surcoats with upturned shoulders. The thighs have mail chausses but the lower legs, unusually, are protected by strips of something very like the later 'penny plate' armour, which consists of small discs held by a rivet through the centre. (By permission of the British Library, MS Royal 2 A XXII, f.220)

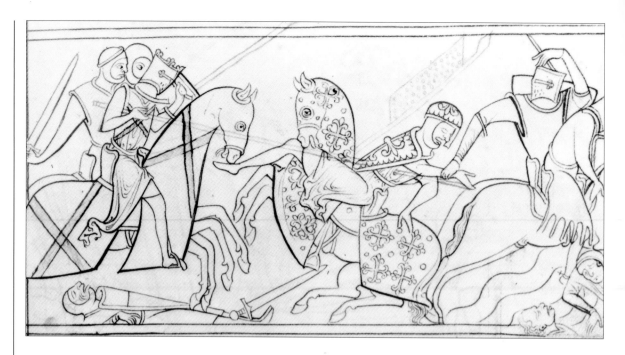

A battle scene from *Lives of the Two Offas*. (By permission of the British Library, MS Cotton Nero D I, f.4)

knights. Unlike in France, the decimal system of organising units in tens, hundreds and thousands seems to have gradually dropped out of use. The loss of such systematic organisation may have something to do with the reduction of effectiveness of horsemen in a co-ordinated charge, and possibly has a bearing on the failure of cavalry in the Scottish conflicts. By 1300 the decimal system had disappeared in England.

Already in the 'Assize of Arms' of 1181, Henry II expected every baron who had a number of knights' fees on his demesne to supply as many sets of hauberks, helmets, shields and lances for them. Henry III's 'Assize' raised the limit to £15 and added a horse to the requirements. Henry III's Assize of 1242 and Edward I's Statute of Winchester in 1285 confirmed the obligation of freemen between the ages of 16 and 60 to perform military service. In 1205, when a French invasion seemed imminent, John called up all freemen over the age of 12, to be organised under constables in their respective hundreds, towns or boroughs. By 1225 even unfree villeins were liable to call up in an emergency, usually being organised by the sheriffs. In the late 13th century, commissioners of array took over. The service, normally paid except within the shire, was usually for 40 days. Infantry were usually divided into units of 100 under a mounted constable. Each unit was subdivided into five units of 20 under an officer called a vintenar, by the end of the century the millenar (who might be a knight, and possibly of the Royal Household) looked after bodies of 1,000 men. Towns also raised militias, that of London suffering particularly on the rebel side at the battle of Lewes.

TRAINING

A candidate for knighthood might well be the son of a knight, though it was possible for a burgess to place an aspiring child. Training began

when about ten years old, though in some cases it could be when as young as seven (reflecting the medieval love of counting in sevens). Often the boy would be sent away to learn his trade, commonly to the household of a relative such as an uncle, though the sons of noble houses might well find themselves at the king's court. As a page, the new recruit would be taught how to behave in polite society, how to keep ladies company, how to sing and dance and recite poetry. However, the boy also needed to begin the tough training that would enable him to survive on the battlefield, and he would start to handle practice weapons and learn about horses. When about 14 years old he graduated to the role of squire, the word derived from the French *ecuyer*, meaning a shield bearer. The youth now trained in earnest with weapons. He cut at the pell or wooden post, wrestled and practised against other squires or knights. When pulled on a wooden horse by comrades, or mounted on a real horse, he tried to keep his seat when his lance rammed the quintain, a post on which was fixed a shield. Some had a pivoting arm, with a shield at one end and a weighted sack at the other; if a strike was made the rider had to pass swiftly by in order to avoid the swinging weight.

Roger of Hoveden, who died about 1201, wrote:

'No athlete can fight tenaciously who has never received any blows: he must see his blood flow and hear his teeth crack under the fist of his adversary, and when he is thrown to the ground he must fight on with all his might and not lose courage … Anyone who can do that can engage in battle confidently.'

The youth came to know how to control the high-spirited stallions that knights rode. He learned to control the horse with his feet and knees when the reins were dropped so he could slip his arm through the **enarmes** of the shield for close combat. He became used to the weight of the mail coat and to the sensation of wearing a helm over mail and padding. He learned

Making a knight, from *Lives of the Two Offas*. His spurs are buckled to his feet and he is belted with his sword, then a mail coat is pulled on while his shield and banner await him. (By permission of the British Library, MS Cotton Nero D I, f.3)

17

ABOVE **In this scene from *Lives of the Two Offas* not only are plate schynbalds and poleyns visible, but also a perhaps unique representation of a face plate without any helmet. (By permission of the British Library, MS Cotton Nero D I, f.7)**

ABOVE **A gilt copper-alloy prick spur of the first half of the 13th century, found in London. The arms are damaged. (By courtesy of the Trustees of the Armouries, VI.380)**

to swing up over the high-backed cantle of the saddle while wearing all his equipment. As well as acquiring these skills, he was now apprenticed to a knight, who might have several squires depending on his status. He had to look after the armour, cleaning mail by kicking it round in a barrel containing sand and vinegar, to scour between the links. Helmets needed polishing and oiling if they were in store. He helped look after the horses, and ordered the knight's baggage.

As he grew older he now also had to follow his lord into battle. In many cases this duty was probably carried out as described in the 13th-century *Rule of the Templars*, where each knight had two squires. On the march they went ahead of the knight, weighed down with equipment and with the led horses. As the knights drew up for battle, one squire stood in front of his master with his lance and shield, the other in rear with the horses. When battle was imminent the first squire passed the lance and shield to his master. The second withdrew with the horses. When the knights charged, the squire riding the spare warhorse followed after his master, to remount him if the first horse was killed or blown. The squire's job was also to extricate his master from the press if wounded.

Some squires were required to care for their lord as a manservant would. The squire learned how to bring in the more important dishes at dinner and to carve them in public. He was taught to hunt in the field, a good exercise, and the arts of falconry and venery, including how to 'break' a kill. To kill deer a squire or knight sometimes handled a bow or, less likely, a crossbow, though he would not use these on the battlefield. Some might be given lessons by a clerk or priest, though many were still illiterate.

Somewhere between the ages of 18 and 21 (the magical multiple of seven again), the successful squire was initiated into the ranks of knighthood. Any knight could bestow this honour but it usually fell to the lord of the squire's household or even the king if the boy was at court. Sometimes knights were made on the battlefield before action, being expected to fight hard to display their skill. Simon de Montfort knighted the young Earl of Leicester and his companions before the battle of Lewes in 1264. Sometimes a squire might be knighted after a battle, a reward for valiant deeds. Usually, however, the process entailed a costly ceremony with all the trimmings, an increasingly onerous burden on many families, since a feast would be expected and perhaps a tournament as well. The Church had by now become inextricably involved with the ideas of chivalry and knighthood, though it could never achieve such a hold over the creation of knights as it had with the crowning of kings, simply because too many knights were of only modest means and could not afford any great proceedings.

A full-blown ceremony would often include many or all of the following elements. The hair and beard (if worn) were trimmed. The day before the ceremony the candidate had a bath, from which he arose clean, a reflection on baptism. He might stand vigil in the chapel all night, his sword laid on the altar, so that he could spend the time in prayer and thoughtful meditation. A bed foreshadowed the place in paradise each knight hoped to win. The young man was then clothed, the meaning of the symbolic colours and accoutrements being explained in a French poem written between 1220 and 1225: a white tunic for purity; a scarlet cloak to represent the blood he is ready to spill in defence of the Church; brown stockings, representing the earth that he will return to in time, an eventuality for which he must always be prepared; a white belt symbolising purity; gilded spurs showing that he would be as swift as a spurred horse in obeying God's commands; the two edges of his sword symbolising justice and loyalty, and the obligation to defend the weak; the cross-guard echoing the cross of Christ. The candidate progressed to the assembled throng, for with no written certificate, even low-key ceremonies needed witnesses. His sword was belted on and spurs set on his feet.

The aspirant was then knighted by a tap on the shoulders with a sword, or perhaps still by the buffet often given previously, a symbolic blow that

A battle scene from *L'Estoire de Seint Aedward le Rei* of *c.*1245. One knight wears a circlet of peacock feathers round his helm, while the king has a simple cervellière. A rather large horseman's spiked axe is also carried. The decorated arçons protrude through slits in the saddle cloths. (Syndics of Cambridge University Library MS EE3. 59, f.32v)

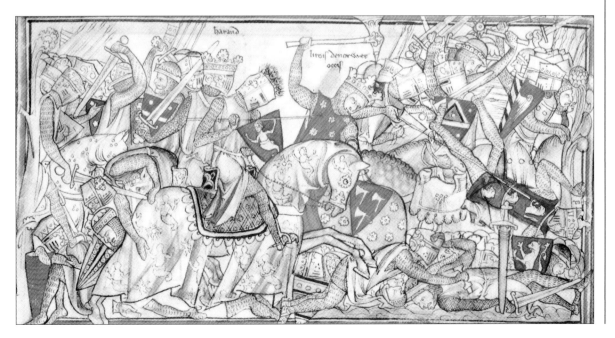

was the only one the new knight had to receive without retaliation. On the other hand it may have symbolised the awakening from evil dreams and henceforth the necessity to keep the faith (as mentioned in a prayer book of 1295). Alternatively it might have been to remember the knight who delivered it. It may even have derived from the habit of boxing the ears of young witnesses to charters to make sure they remembered the occasion, but it is not certain. Words of encouragement and wisdom were exchanged, along the lines of protecting the Church, the poor, the weak and women, and refraining from treason. The new knight then displayed his prowess, sometimes in a tournament, and there was celebrating. A number of squires were sometimes knighted together.

Magna Carta has a clause confirming that the king and magnates could ask their tenants for a sum to defray the costs of knighting their eldest sons. It was these expenses, plus the rights and services expected of knights, that drove many to avoid knighthood altogether and led to its subsequent enforcement through laws of distraint. In 1204, for example, King John spent £33 on 'three robes of scarlet and three of green, two baldekins, one mattress and other necessities for making one knight'. He also knighted one of his valets, Thomas Esturmi, that same year but spent only £6 10s on the latter's robes: 'A scarlet robe and a hood of deerskin, another green or brown robe, a saddle, a harness, a rain-cape, a mattress and a pair of linen sheets'. In 1248 William de Plessetis is told to send 'one silk robe, two linen robes, a cape and a bed and other things necessary to the making of a knight'.

New knights continued their training in the same way as they had when squires, since they were expected to be able to fight well when required.

ARMOUR AND WEAPONS

The commonest body armour of the 13th-century knight was **mail**, consisting of interlinked iron rings made up into garments. Despite the amount of mail that was undoubtedly in use, little has survived in any quantity dating from before the late 14th or early 15th centuries and none of that which does survive is of English manufacture. For the most part we are thrown back on manuscript illustrations and sculpted figures to reconstruct the knight of the period.

Hugh de Boves flees at the battle of Bouvines in 1214, from the *Chronica majora of Matthew Paris*, c.1250. (The Master and Fellows of Corpus Christi College, Cambridge, MS 16, f.37r)

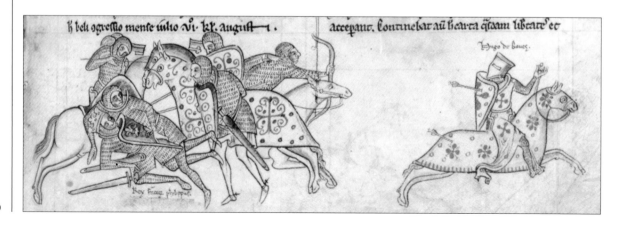

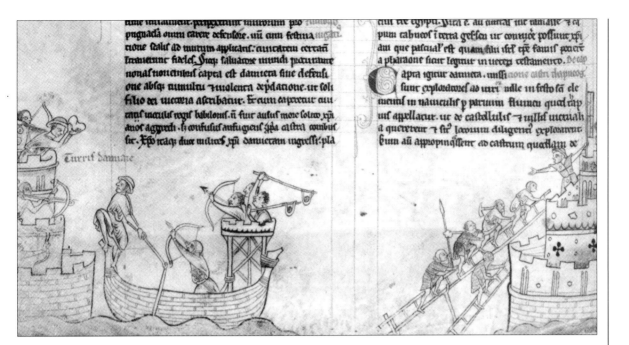

The siege of Damietta in 1219, showing a staff sling in use, from the *Chronica majora*, c.1250. William Longespée was present with other English crusaders. (The Master and Fellows of Corpus Christi College, Cambridge, MS 16, f.55v)

The process by which mail was made has largely been lost but certain procedures must have been necessary. First wire would be drawn through a board with holes of varying diameter to arrive at the correct thickness. The wire was then wound round a rod and cut down one side to produce individual rings. Each was flattened at the ends to allow a tiny hole to be pierced, before being interlinked with four other rings. The open ends were overlapped and secured by hammering a tiny rivet through the two holes. This process had to be done thousands of times to produce a single coat. It is likely that a workshop included men who drew wire and cut out the rings ready for assembly, this being done by the mailmaker. It required a knowledge of how to add or subtract rings to expand or narrow a garment and to allow an arm to be lowered without bunching in the armpit. The finished garment might be case-hardened by packing charcoal around it in a charcoal fire. Whether special tools were produced to speed up the process is not known for certain. In some cases alternate lines of riveted and welded rings may have been used, but it was far more usual for all rings to be riveted .

The mail coat was called a **hauberk**. This was usually about knee-length or a little shorter, split up the fork a short distance to facilitate riding, with wrist-length sleeves extended over the hands to form mail **mufflers**, or mittens. The neck was extended up to form a hood. To guard the throat the slit below the chin, which facilitated putting on the coat, might be laced shut. However, it was more common to extend one side of the lower edge of the hood as a flap of mail that could be drawn up across the chin and often the mouth when action was expected. This was called a **ventail**, and was probably usually lined or padded for comfort. In order to secure it in place a lace, threaded through the rings at the temple to keep the hood in place, was tied through the rings on the ventail. Some were fitted instead with a buckle to secure through a strap, or possibly a hook. A padded and quilted coif or cap was worn under the mail, tied under the chin with laces. By about

1275 some knights had begun to wear a separate coif but integral coifs remained equally if not more popular throughout the rest of the century.

A mail coat weighed roughly 30 pounds, depending on its length and the thickness of the rings. Some slightly shorter versions were also seen, with three-quarter or elbow-length sleeves, and are very probably the form known as a **haubergeon**.

In about 1250 Matthew Paris depicts a cuffed **gauntlet** made separately from the sleeve of the mail coat, but such an item was rare until the following century. At this date it appears to have been a form of bag gauntlet of leather with a flaring cuff, or a form reinforced by whalebone or metal plates inside or outside a leather or canvas mitten.

The legs were covered by **chausses** (mail stockings), fitted with leather soles to aid grip and braced up to a belt at the waist, rather like the cloth stockings worn underneath. A leather belt was probably used to anchor them with ties, rather than bracing them to the girdle of the **braies** (drawers). A further tie laced through the links below the knee might be used to prevent sagging. Sometimes a strip of mail was worn over the front of the leg and foot instead, this being secured with lacing and presumably held up in a similar fashion to a waist belt.

By about 1225 the **gamboised cuisse** appeared to protect the thigh and knee, and took the form of a quilted padded tube, presumably tied to the same belt as the chausses. By mid-century small cup-shaped pieces called **genouilliers** (also known as **poleyns**) were occasionally worn over the knees, either attached directly to the mail chausses or else over the gamboised cuisses. At first they were small but soon larger versions appeared that wrapped around the sides of the knee as well. Some may have been made from *cuir bouilli* (a hard but light material made by moulding leather that has been boiled or soaked in water or oil) and they may have been laced or stitched in place or else riveted through the mail. Very rarely, a similar small cup-shaped piece was seen at

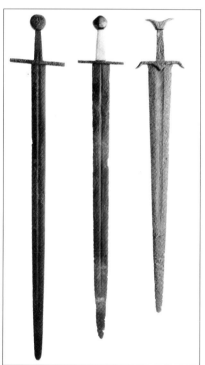

ABOVE **The left sword dates to the first half of the 13th century. The middle sword is probably of the 12th century but might still have been worn in the 13th. The right-hand weapon dates to the second half of the 13th century and is similar to the type seen on the great seal of Edward I. (By courtesy of the Trustees of the Armouries, IX.1027, 1082, 1107)**

the elbow. Shin defences, called **schynbalds**, were simple gutter-shaped plates strapped around the leg over the mail.

It is likely that a padded tunic, known as the **aketon** (from the Arabic *al-qutun* for 'cotton'), **wambais**, **pourpoint** or **gambeson**, was worn under the mail. Though mail moves easily, its very flexibility means that a powerful blow can result in bruising or even broken bones without the links being torn. If mail links were cut, they could be driven back into the wound, increasing the likelihood of septicaemia. In the early 13th century Guillaume le Breton, writing of a fight some years before between William de Barres and the future Richard I, describes the lances piercing shield, hauberk and aketon. Gerald de Barri, writing in the late 12th century, mentions a leather tunic worn under mail, which may have been an alternative to an aketon. Padded aketons seem to have consisted of two layers of cotton stuffed with wool, cotton, old rags or similar, and held in place by vertical, or occasionally trellis, stitching. Later versions are known to have been made from numerous thicknesses of linen, and this may have been an alternative style. Some examples worn by infantry in illustrations in the mid-13th century French *Maciejowski Bible* seem to have inset sleeves, since nowhere do they vary in colour to suggest a sleeved coat over a sleeveless version (although gambesons are sometimes referred to as being worn over an aketon). However, it is not known if examples worn beneath mail were similar. Some gambesons, perhaps those mentioned as made of silks and other rich materials, were occasionally worn over mail and, at the end of the century, over the coat of plates.

Richard Marshal unhorses Baldwin of Gynes at Monmouth in 1233, from the *Chronica majora*, *c.*1250. (The Master and Fellows of Corpus Christi College, Cambridge, MS 16, f.85r)

In a few instances a mail coat is shown with a long flowing garment issuing from below the hem, in much the same way as was seen in the 12th century. This is far too fluid to be a padded coat, and in any case is also occasionally seen under civilian tunics.

The description by Guillaume le Breton also mentions a plate of worked iron worn under the aketon, presumably over the heart. No illustration of such a defence is known. However, by mid-century, glimpses of additional body defence begin to appear. An effigy at Pershore Abbey in Worcestershire and another in the Temple Church, London, show that some form of breast- and back-plates are buckled over the mail but under the surcoat. It is not known whether iron, steel or *cuir bouilli* is intended. Examples of some form of leather body armour, the **cuirie**, with or without additional metal pieces, appear to be worn by infantrymen in several 13th-century manuscripts, laced at about two points down the side.

It is possible that the upwardly curved shoulders seen in the *Maciejowski Bible* example and some instances of surcoats with similar shoulders may be explained by some form of leather armour, though this shape could equally be achieved by stiffening the surcoat material. The inventory of Fawkes de Bréauté of 1224 mentions 'an espaulier' of black cendal silk (a silk textile ressembling coarse sarsenet), perhaps a padded shoulder piece of some kind. It is also possible that a large upper chest piece or collar produced the shaped shoulder. However, collars of a certain form do appear on a number of illustrations, worn over the mail or else beneath, visible when the ventail is loosed and the coif is flung back on the shoulders. They appear to be covered in cloth but it is not clear if they are of iron or whalebone, as sometimes mentioned; a few may simply be quilted. Equally it is not clear if they are all separate or whether some were attached to the aketon, as shown when worn by footsoldiers. It is not known how they articulated, but it seems that they either fastened at both sides or hinged on the wearer's left and were laced on the right side. At the end of the century a plate defence for the chin and neck, the gorget or bevor, was known in France and possibly England.

The surcoat was a cloth garment worn over armour. It appears to have been introduced in the second quarter of the 12th century and was increasingly popular by the early 13th century, though even towards mid-century by no means all knights wore one. The length varied from above the knee down to the ankles, and the skirts were split front and rear almost up to the waist for ease in riding. Its main purpose is not clear, suggestions varying from keeping the armour dry or out of sunlight, to copying Muslim fashion or for displaying heraldry. The latter is the least persuasive: the surcoat was frequently left in a single colour which appears to bear little relation to a family's coat-of-arms. As for other aspects of their design, most appear to have been lined in a contrasting colour. They were usually secured at the waist by a plaited cord or decorative belt, which also helped to hitch up the mail beneath and ease the weight on the shoulders. A few surcoats may have been lined over the chest with plates.

A new item of equipment evolved in mid-century. The **coat of plates** was a poncho-style garment pulled on over the head, with side panels that wrapped over the back flap where they were tied or buckled. The front and sides were lined with large rectangular plates, presumably either of iron or whalebone, the rivet heads visible on the outside. By the end of the century many English documents mention the coat of plates, or plates as it is often called, over the mail but under the surcoat. It is not known if variants seen in the following century, such as those opening at the sides or shoulder, or constructed with smaller plates, were used at this time.

Scale armour was still worn occasionally, though was by no means as popular as mail. It is sometimes represented in art, but when it does appear it is commonly allocated to Saracens or other groups, as though to distinguish them from the western knights. It was constructed from small scales of iron, copper-alloy, whalebone or leather, attached to a cloth or leather backing so that the scales overlapped downwards, like those of a fish.

Several varieties of helmet were in use. The conical form was either raised from a single piece of iron or steel, sometimes with reinforcing bands, or else made in the form of the old Germanic *spangenhelm*, from four segments riveted inside a framework of iron bands, usually four springing from a brow band. Such helmets would still be seen in mid-century, but in art they are sometimes ascribed to the 'baddies', emphasising the more up-to-date equipment of the 'good guys'. By 1200 round and cylindrical variants were already popular. All three forms might have a **nasal**, but are sometimes provided with a

An English ivory chess-piece of c.1250 carved in the shape of a mounted knight with sword, shield and flat-topped helm. (Ashmolean Museum, Oxford)

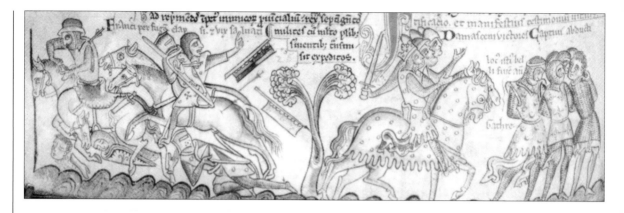

face mask. A few had a neck-guard, and in the late 12th century the two were joined to produce a rudimentary form of the **great helm**. This form, rare in 1200, was usually shallower at the rear than at the front, though the second seal of Richard I suggests that helms reaching the same depth all round were known before 1200.

The all-enclosing **helm** became increasingly popular through the 13th century. Some had a single vision slit across the front, and gradually reinforcing bars were added to strengthen the metal around the slits and down the medial line at the front. The front plates overlapped those in the rear to afford a smoother surface against a weapon point. The flat top was riveted over the upper edges. This form of top surface was much less protective than conical or even round-topped helmets, but nevertheless remained the usual form until later in the century. After about 1250 the upper sides began to taper, though the top usually remained flat. From about 1275 a few tapered to a point and by the end of the century round-topped examples were also seen. The lower edges had also deepened and by 1300 the first visors may have appeared.

By mid-century the **cervellière** (also known at this date as a **basinet**), a small, hemispherical skull cap of iron, had become popular and increasingly supplanted the conical and round-topped helmets. Sometimes worn over the mail hood but under the helm, illustrations reveal that it could also be worn under the hood but over the padded coif, and would account for a number of pictures showing warriors apparently wearing very rounded coifs and seemingly no other head defence. Such hoods often show a lace around the temples, either to keep the mail in place or also to help secure the cervellière.

All helmets were fitted with a padded lining, though representations at this date are virtually non-existent. Surviving 14th-century linings and representations in art suggest linings were typically of canvas padded with horsehair, tow, wool, grass or something similar, either glued inside the helmet, or else secured by stitching to a line of small holes along the helmet rim, or else to a leather or canvas band riveted inside the brim, the band held by crude square or rectangular washers. The upper part was probably scalloped and a draw string threaded through the top ends of each scallop to adjust for fit. This was particularly important once the face was covered, since the vision slits needed to align with the eyes whenever the helmet was donned. The lining of a great helm did not extend down over the face plates, as this would cover the ventilation holes. Helmets were laced or occasionally buckled in place under the chin; laces (some probably bifurcated) were secured either to one of the rivets or else to a flattened hook or loop inside the brim. Manuscript illustrations and references show that some helmets were painted.

In the later 12th century helmet crests had appeared, usually on the helm – Richard I is shown with one on his second seal. The fan crest was sometimes made from thin metal, though wood and parchment were also used, especially for tournament versions. The fan could be painted with the coat-of-arms or some part of it. Three-dimensional crests were also sometimes used, made from whalebone or, more commonly, wood, parchment or leather.

A shield was carried since this provided a solid defence as opposed to the flexible defence of the mail coat. Made from wooden planks and faced with leather or parchment, most were probably lined with parchment, cloth or leather as well. No English shield from this period survives, and continental examples come from churches, perhaps being specially made for this purpose, so it is not certain that coverings such as gesso and moulding would usually have been used on war-shields. The wood tends to be about 0.6in. thick. There are usually three **brases** or **enarmes** (carrying straps) riveted through to the front; illustrations sometimes show buckles to adjust their length. In order to prevent bruising to the forearm a pad was nailed between the straps. In addition, a **guige strap** allowed the shield to hang from the neck (or with only the forearm through the brases) in the charge or to prevent loss in battle, or allow the shield to be strapped to the back or hung up when not in use. Rarely a buckler, a small circular wooden shield with a central metal boss over a hand grip, may have been used.

An indenture for the hire of a suit of armour, dated 1282, mentions an aketon, haubergeon, collar, basinet, a pair of whalebone gauntlets, a pair of mustiliers and of cuisses, and a cendal silk tunic of arms. Valued at 6 marks, this expensive equipment was probably for the Welsh Wars but the indenture also noted that the armour was to be returned in good condition!

Horsemen lay about them, from the *Douce Apocalypse* of about 1250. Note the mail mittens pushed back from the hands of the central figure who wears a kettle hat. Two riders wield falchions, that on the left rather fanciful. (The Bodleian Library, University of Oxford, MS Douce 180, f.31)

Tournament armour was also starting to evolve at this time, though in a much less noticeable form than later. The Purchase Roll for the Windsor Tournament of 1278 mentions leather cuirasses with buckram sleeves, *cuir bouilli* helms painted silver, with similar shaffrons for the horses. Aillettes are tied with silken cords. Cendal silk surcoats were worn. Whalebone swords were covered in parchment and silvered and their hilts gilded. There is no mention of lances, so this was presumably a form of **behourd** (see page 45) with

blunt weapons. Another reference in 1204 mentions linen armour but with lances, suggesting the use of a form of thickly padded aketon, perhaps of numerous layers of linen.

Weapons

As in other centuries, the prized weapon was the sword. In the early years of the century the sword was essentially a cutting weapon, divided into five major types. Some blades had straight, razor-sharp edges running almost parallel to a sharp point, with a fuller (or channel) down the centre of each side of the blade, to lighten it. Another form was more tapered, the fuller running perhaps three-quarters of the way down; this would become the commonest form of sword until the third quarter of the 13th century, and some were large specimens. In about 1240 a new type of sword appeared, broad-bladed, often widening slightly towards the grip, which was often about 6 inches long, though narrower blades and shorter grips were also seen in the second half of the century. The fuller usually reached about halfway down the blade. Larger versions of this form had blades from about 37 to 40 inches in length, the grip rising to perhaps 9 inches. These, like the larger swords mentioned previously, were great swords or swords of war, also later known as bastard or hand-and-a-half swords. It may be that the gradual increase in solid body armour and limb defences was the reason for the development of a short, wide-bladed slashing sword that nevertheless tapered to a sharp point. The fuller on these ran about half-way, and it always seems to be provided with some form of wheel pommel at the end of a usually short grip. In about 1280 a strongly tapered acutely pointed sword of flattened siamond section made its appearance

Pommel forms varied. The plain or chamfered variety of disc pommels were perhaps the commonest forms, though a wheel type with a pronounced form of centre was known but not particularly common until the second half of the century. A rare type, shaped like a petalled flower, was in use from about 1280. A version of the old 'cocked hat' Viking pommel was in use mainly in the middle 50 years of the century, and a diamond version was also seen until about 1275. Another throwback had indented top edges and is found largely on northern English and southern Scottish monuments dating from about 1250 onwards. Rarely, spherical pommels were seen, or perhaps a low boat-shaped type.

The cross-guard was often fairly simple, sometimes curving slightly towards the blade. The tang was covered by a wooden

Warriors on foot, that on the left with a stiffened collar. A number wear gamboised cuisses and poleyns. (The Bodleian Library, University of Oxford, MS Douce 180, f.87)

grip formed from two halves carved out for the tang and glued together, usually further bound with leather and sometimes by leather or silk cords, perhaps mixed with silver or gold wire. Scabbards were made from wooden boards, covered in leather and fitted with an iron or copper-alloy chape at the tip. Some had a metal locket at the mouth. The sword belt became an ingenious arrangement of cut and interlaced straps designed to hold the sword at a convenient angle for drawing and to prevent the owner tripping over it. At the beginning of the century belts were forked at one end and tied by passing these through two slots cut in the side attached to the scabbard, before knotting them together. By mid-century a strap and buckle arrangement had become usual, the strap ending in a metal finial. Belts were often decorated, perhaps with gilt eyelets and bars.

An unusual form of sword that appeared in the 13th century was the **falchion**, in shape not unlike a butcher's cleaver. Instead of being designed to balance as close to the hand as possible, it had a short blade that was wider and heavier towards the point, to produce a powerful cutting weapon.

Daggers were sometimes worn, though seldom are the sheaths shown in art, even when knights are holding the weapon. The blades tapered to a point but otherwise the hilt tended to resemble that of a small sword; the short cross-guard seems in some cases to have curled in tightly towards the blade. Surviving leather knife sheaths are often embossed with designs.

Armourers at work, hammering a helm and checking a sword, watched by a mailed horse, from the *Roman de toute chevalerie* of Thomas of Kent, *c.*1250. (Reproduced by permission of the Master and Fellows of Trinity College Cambridge, MS 0.9.34, f.24r)

The **lance** was carried by horsemen, a straight wooden staff, often of ash, tipped with a socketed steel head nailed on to the shaft. There does not appear to have been any form of vamplate to defend the hand until the 14th century. Already for jousts of peace in the tournament some blunted heads were in use, and some form of **coronel**, a head formed of three or more points to spread the force of a blow, may have been used.

The mace was sometimes carried, though it was not as popular as it would be when plate armour began to proliferate. The haft was made of wood, and in the early years the head tended to be a moulded copper-alloy knob covered in projections. By mid-century flanged forms were also in use, usually with parallel sides. A wrist strap might be bound round the haft. The military flail for horsemen appeared by the end of the 13th century, a spiked ball chained to a haft, but was not common.

Other weapons were sometimes carried. A long-handled axe with a trumpet-shaped head could be used on foot and, surprisingly, is also sometimes seen being wielded by horsemen, occasionally fitted with a rear spike. A more convenient form for the rider was a short horseman's axe with a rear spike, in form rather like a tomahawk or modern fireman's axe. Another two-handed weapon also occasionally shown in use on horseback is the **glaive**, consisting of a long convex blade mounted on a haft.

Flags took several forms. The **pennon** or **pennoncelle** was a small triangular flag nailed to the lance behind the head, and was painted with the owner's arms. Bannerets had a banner, at this time usually a slim rectangular flag with the longest side against the staff, where it was nailed or tied in place. Banners bore their owner's arms and were carried by banner bearers whose duty was to stay close to their lord.

The lord's arms at this period could also be carried by all his followers. In 1218 a robber is recorded buying 100 marks worth of cloth for his band as though he were a baron or earl, suggesting that followers could be equipped in coats of the same colour at least. Barons and knights had the right to have their knights and squires wear a badge or uniform.

Horse furniture

Horses were sometimes covered in a **trapper** or **caparison**, a cloth housing coming down to the hocks and sometimes covering the tail. These were often divided into two parts at the saddle, but illustrations occasionally show trappers that appear to be made in one piece. They were usually extended to form a head covering, sometimes with shaped ear coverings. In some instances the whole trapper was probably quilted. It was increasingly used to display the arms of the rider, although many were plain. By the end of the century illustrations often show the shield and trapper carrying the coat-of-arms, while the surcoat is plain. Trappers appear to have had linings, perhaps as separate items to absorb the horse's sweat, though illustrations suggest they were integral. By mid-century some illustrations show trappers made from mail, which must have been supported by a quilted trapper beneath or else a

A good representation of a mail coat complete with integral hood and mittens, from the *Roman de toute chevalerie* of Thomas of Kent, *c.*1250. Note there is no evidence of an aketon underneath, though the hatched lining could just represent a quilted lining. One horse wears a mail trapper. (Reproduced by permission of the Master and Fellows of Trinity College Cambridge, MS 0.9.34, f.17v)

linen lining, as probably described in the inventory of Fawkes de Bréauté of 1224, where mail and linen are mentioned together. In 1277, 16 shillings was paid for two linen coverings to go under the mail. Such trappers covered the whole horse except the ears. Squires in Edward I's army were expected to ride 'covered' horses, and if they did not, their wages fell to 6d or 8d. Since their animals were **rounceys** worth about £5–£8, rather than powerful war-horses, does 'covered' refer to cloth or quilted trappers, or even perhaps those made from *cuir bouilli*?

The seal of Robert FitzWalter shows the neck and head of a horse covered with trellis patterning, as though this area is quilted. Separate versions of these hoods, probably those referred to as **testiers**, are sometimes seen towards the end of the century. **Shaffrons** are not illustrated although leather forms are mentioned in the Windsor Tournament Roll of 1278, and they appear on some continental illustrations.

Civilian dress

Basic dress was much the same at all levels of society, but the cut and materials varied with the rank of the wearer. Undergarments consisted of a linen shirt with wrist-length sleeves, and a pair of linen drawers or **braies**. The braies came down to the knee or below, the loose ends sometimes being turned back and tied to the draw-string at the waist, which emerged at intervals. Over the shirt came a **tunic**, again with wrist-length sleeves, that virtually hid the shirt. Knee-length tunics were common, but ankle-length versions might be worn by men of rank and on formal occasions. Both types were usually slit up to the girdle at front and rear. Tunics were provided with a short vertical slit at the neck closed with a brooch or pin, or sometimes with a low neck, to allow them to be pulled on. Less commonly diagonal slits from neck to chest, or horizontally to the shoulder, were seen. More rarely than in previous centuries, embroidered bands of woven or appliqué decoration might be added at neck, wrist, hem or occasionally the upper arm, or an all-over pattern used, more likely on long tunics. Many, however, were of a single colour, though the cloth might be lined in an alternate colour. The sleeves in this century were often of magyar form, that is, made in one with the body with a wide armhole often reaching the waist, tapering to a tight cuff.

Over the tunic might be worn a variety of **super-tunics**, also called **surcoats**. Some were similar to those worn the previous century, either the same length as the tunic or a little shorter, with either tight or loose sleeves, the latter sometimes elbow-length or, rarely, with pendulous cuffs. Some were worn with a girdle. The **pelisson** was a super-tunic lined with fur. Fashion-conscious males, however, wore a variety of new super-tunics. The **tabard** was rather like a poncho put on over the head, the sides either stitched at waist level or clasped. The front was often slit up to match the side openings, but no belt was worn. The

The battle of Hastings in 1066, as visualised by a 13th-century artist. (By permission of the British Library, MS Vitellius A XIII, f.3b)

garde-corps or **herygoud** was a bulky coat reaching shins or ankles, with wide tubular sleeves gathered at the shoulders and reaching beyond the hands; long slits in the front of the sleeve allowed the arm to pass through. The garde-corps was usually hooded, and worn without a belt. From about 1260 a loose super-tunic with wide sleeves reaching just below the elbows might be worn, sometimes with a belt. At about the same time the **garnache** appeared, rather like the tabard but with very wide shoulders, while the sides could be stitched below waist level, or from waist to hem, or simply left open. It, too, was beltless. Some wore a belted sleeveless surcoat similar to that worn over armour. From *c.*1250 those super-tunics with no side opening were provided with vertical slits called fitchets, allowing access to the purse or keys if carried on the tunic girdle.

The legs were covered by stockings. Short ones reached the knee and might have an ornamental border. Longer versions reached mid-thigh and were pulled over the drawers. They ended in a tongue and were secured by a tie to the girdle of the drawers. Some had a stirrup instead of feet, while others were footed with a leather sole, this type being made of wool or occasionally of thin leather. Some were gartered below the knee, and for a short period around 1200 cross-gartering over the whole leg was sometimes used by noblemen. Shoes were often plain and shaped to the ankle, with inner lacing or buckles. Others were open over the foot and cut high behind the ankle, or open over the foot and closed by an ankle or instep strap. Loose boots (buskins) were sometimes worn, often being quite short.

Cloaks were sometimes worn, being rectangular or semicircular and reaching anywhere from the knee to the ankle; some were hooded. They were fastened in the centre or on the left shoulder to allow free movement of the right arm and secured by an ornamental brooch or clasp, or else by drawing one top corner of the cloak through a ring sewn to the other corner, then knotting the end. They were made from various materials, richer cloth being used by the nobility, who tended to wear longer versions. Cloaks were often lined with fur, one such version being quite small.

As well as hoods, which might be buttoned, other forms of headgear were worn. There was a cap called a **hure**, stalked round caps, and large brimmed hats for travelling, sometimes with the brim turned up at the back or worn reversed with the turned-up brim to the front. Some round-crowned hats (that might have a knob on top) had down-turned brims, rolled brims or those like bowler hats. The coif was similar to that

The knights in this scene from the *Trinity Apocalypse* of *c.*1250–60 display a number of interesting features. The king in the foreground is wearing poleyns and schynbalds that appear unconnected to each other. Despite this up-to-date plate armour he only wears a strip of mail beneath, instead of full mail chausses. His saddle has a double girth for extra strength, and two of the cantles are painted with arms. His breast-band supports decorative shield-shaped pendants. The high shoulder on the surcoats may suggest a cuirie, though only the lining is visible, prompting the conclusion that the cloth was stiffened. Both kings appear to be left-handed (though the scabbards are also on the left side) but this is probably a stylistic design to prevent the shield obscuring them. The shields all have borders, unlike many of those shown by Matthew Paris. One rider has a kettle hat. (Reproduced by permission of the Master and Fellows of Trinity College Cambridge, MS R.16.2, f.23r)

A: Knight c.1210

B B: The hunt

C: Horses

GRAHAM TURNER '01

C

D: Magna Carta

E: Knight c.1250

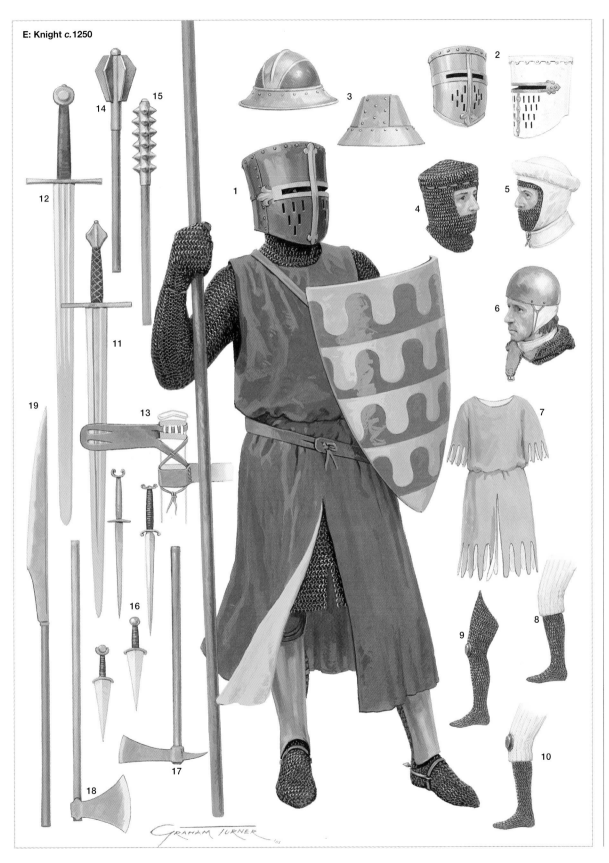

H: Knight c.1290

used with armour, though unpadded. Hair was worn with a fringe or centre parting and was waved to the nape of the neck; beards and moustaches were not overly long. Young men tended to be clean-shaven, and bobbed their hair, with a fringe or roll curl across the forehead and at the nape, which appeared below the coif when one was worn.

Gloves were sometimes worn by the nobility, some almost elbow-length, and often decorated with a broad band of gold embroidery down the back to the knuckles. Buttons were used for ornamentation. The rich used expensive materials such as silks; baudekin or siclaton was a silk cloth with a warp of gold thread. Byssine was a fine cotton or flax material, burnet a brown cloth. Cotton was at this time a woollen imitation of continental cotton cloths.

IDEALS AND CUSTOMS

Chivalry

Binding knights together was chivalry, from *cheval*, the French word for a horse. By the 13th century the connection with riding had expanded to include a whole range of other ideas. The Church had done its best to harness the violence of the warrior class, by imposing the Peace and then the Truce of God from the 11th century, but this had only met with marginal success. Nevertheless it steered knights into crusades for the glory of God and invoked their protection for the weak and for women. The cult of the Virgin had appeared in France during the 12th century, as had the love poetry of the southern French troubadours, which then moved north to find a less heady form among the trouvères of northern France. Also in the 12th century tales of King Arthur grew more widely known, supported by the English kings who, as foreigners themselves, were keen to associate with a native English hero. These romances were a blend of adventure, love, monsters and magic. The sub-Roman Arthur became a medieval knight, his court echoed in the social gatherings called Round Tables held by English kings. The romances showed how knights should behave, as brave and bold adventurers, seeking the Holy Grail that only the purest would attain.

Reality, of course, was often far different. Marriages were usually hard bargains, a matter of lands, dowries and marriage portions, and girls were often betrothed when only ten years old or less. Not a few knights were quite happy to let someone else do the fighting. But chivalry bound this stratum of society together, and the exclusivity attached to it seems to have increased during the 13th century, perhaps reflected in the appearance of knightly effigies. The social divisions in England after the Norman Conquest had been diluted by intermarriage, enough for Orderic Vitalis in the 12th century to remark that it was difficult to tell apart freemen of the different races. The court language would remain

A rare early picture of war-horses fighting, from an English bestiary of about 1255. It is sometimes thought that stallions were trained to use their natural aggression but actual evidence is difficult to find, especially from this period. Their riders meanwhile battle it out on foot. (By permission of the British Library, MS Royal 12 F XIII, f.42v)

French until at least the 14th century, and the more cultured could read Latin, though most were still illiterate, and proud of it. They ate few green vegetables (considered food for peasants) but large amounts of meat, with fish on Fridays. Men of standing validated documents with their personal seals, usually depicting them in armour on their war-horses.

The poetry and romances often depict the heroes as men of matchless courage, slaying left and right. It has been pointed out, however, that knights in real war reacted to combat as most men will in any age. They felt braver than others might do because they were well-armoured (though this was by no means proof against all weapons). They advanced in close formation partly because there was safety in numbers and it was reassuring to be pressed up close with comrades. The ideals of honour and steadfastness under the eyes of friends kept men at their station, but such bravery might evaporate and knights slip away or be involved in the infectious panic that turned into flight.

England was a Catholic country and, where possible, knights heard Mass daily. All castles were equipped with a chapel of some description, from small workmanlike structures to beautifully decorated affairs. The Church always tried to take its part in everyday life, and it was useful for fighting men to have God's ear; those in peril of death were often keen to make confession before risking their life. In the field a sword's cross-guard made a suitable crucifix, especially if the sword had been blessed on the altar.

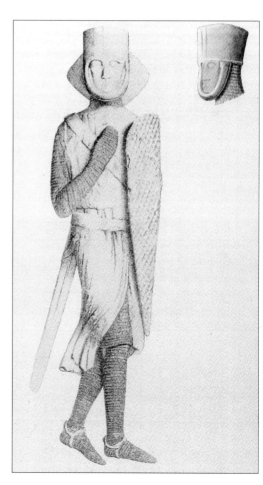

All the same it is hard to accept that some of the more brutal mercenaries had much care for Christian beliefs. The Flemish mercenaries of King John were hated for their cold callousness. The Scots who raided into Cumbria and Northumberland after Wallace's victory at Stirling Bridge killed men, women and children, causing an outcry that suggests this was not considered normal practice in England. The *Chronicon de Lanercost* relates that Hugh de Cressingham, killed at Stirling Bridge, had his skin stripped off to make a sword belt for Wallace.

Inheritance and tax

The rule of primogeniture meant that a man's inheritance usually passed to his eldest son, thus leaving large numbers of landless younger sons, some of whom went into the Church. Many, however, went off to seek their fortune, hoping for employment in the retinues of other lords. When an eldest son came into his inheritance he had to pay his lord a relief, a sort of death duty or fine for permission to receive his father's lands. Magna Carta laid down that this should be £100 for a barony and 100 shillings for a knight's fee. If a lord

LEFT **The seal of John de Warenne, Earl of Surrey, c.1254. Typical of the seals used by high-ranking nobles, it also shows his surcoat and horse's trapper covered in his arms – chequy or and azure (gold and blue). (By permission of the British Library, Seals LXXX 66)**

BELOW LEFT **Effigy of c.1250–60 in the Temple Church, London, sometimes attributed to Geoffrey de Mandeville. The presumed difficulty of removing such a helmet has led to suggestions that the chin defence is simply a pad, or a thick lace tie (unlikely on a detailed effigy) or else a padded arming cap with chin pad. The latter is unlikely since reinforcing bands are in evidence around the helmet, Stothard shows it as grey, and similar helmets are also seen on a late 12th/early 13th century scene of the murder of Becket.**

BELOW **Detail of the helmet.**

had no son, his inheritance was split between his daughters. If they were not heiresses, a lord's daughters were sometimes married off to his knights, but the latter, when marriage was the easiest way to advancement and wealth, might well need an incentive such as a cash payment, land or a reduction in their knight service. Under-age heirs who became orphans were made the wards of their lord or king, who usually milked their estates for every financial gain possible.

There were certain occasions when a lord could demand an 'aid' from his free tenants to meet some very heavy expenditure. Magna Carta limited this burden to ransoming the lord himself, knighting his eldest son or marrying his eldest daughter for the first time. Not until the Statute of Westminster in 1275 was a financial limit set on how much could be demanded in an aid, at 20 shillings for each knight's fee or £20 worth of land held at a rent.

Distraint of knighthood

Civil duties for knights increased during the century. In the courts of the lord's honour they received experience of law and business. In shire and hundred courts they had the opportunity to become involved with local government. They also oversaw the venison in royal forests and forest pasture-rights. Knights of the shire were expected to sit in judgement, at least in the juries of Grand Assize (for land settlements, including on-site inspections), and often in others. Suspected felons might be placed under the custody of a group of knights until called. There always seem to have been enough knights to fulfil these duties, even when after the revolt against John and the accession of Henry III, rebels returned to their allegiances. Common writs were produced to allow such men, for a price, to buy back lands they had previously held. All this required juries of knights, and the pressure of work grew appreciably. Men eligible for knighthood began to avoid it.

What worried the king, however, was not the loss of jury members but the loss of men in armour. In 1224 everyone in possession of a knight's fee was ordered to become a knight by Easter of the following year. This process was distraint of knighthood, an attempt to increase the number of knights by force. In 1234 the king ordered that all those holding one or more knights' fees directly (in chief) from the king should get some armour and be knighted, but he rather undermined this by granting exemptions to certain people in return for cash. In 1241 another order was sent out, this time to anyone holding land worth £20 per year. Further demands were made in the 1250s, including one in 1254 in which the king's son figured. In 1282 all those with £30 of land were instructed to equip themselves with a horse and armour (though they did not actually have to be knights), and in 1285 all freeholders worth more than £100 per year were required to be knighted. This qualification fell in 1292 to all those with £40. From 1294 wealth alone became the qualification for service, not knighthood.

Whether or not there was a so-called 'crisis of the gentry' in the 13th century is heavily debated by

historians; certainly a number of men of knightly rank found life hard, and distraint a nuisance, when there were plenty of mounted troops available who were not technically knights. Pay had now risen from 8d a day for a knight to 2 shillings, and 4 shillings for a banneret, but thereafter stayed the same until the 15th century. The monarch also tried to attract new knights by making the ceremony of knighthood more special and by knighting groups of candidates together. Edward I also used Round Tables and tournaments as a lure to knighthood, harking back to Arthurian and other romances as a stimulant.

Tournaments and Round Tables

Many knights enjoyed **tournaments**, but the idea had been looked on in England with suspicion. In 1204, however, King John provided money for two of his foreign mercenaries to buy linen armour, presumably for tournament use. In 1215 tournaments were used as the occasions for meetings of the barons, such as that at Staines staged while the barons held London and waited for French assistance. The Church had always been against tournaments because of their violence and threatened

Stothard's drawing of an effigy of about 1250–60 in the Temple Church, London, wearing a tight arming cap over his mail, with a rolled pad for a helm. Another figure of the second quarter of the century has a 'balaclava-like' form also covering the neck.

excommunication on participants, but in 1219 even the presence of the Archbishop of Canterbury failed to stop the proceedings at Staines. Henry III also relaxed the ban until the rebellion of Richard Marshal. Illicit tournaments continued to be held in addition. One at Blyth in 1237 between northerners and southerners ended in an all-out battle and the papal legate was needed to quell the ill feeling. Even so the violent contests continued, with trouble fuelled by the enmity between the discontented barons under Henry III and his French favourites. In 1248 William de Valence was soundly beaten with clubs but wreaked his revenge at Brackley a year later. The French knights were beaten in 1251 at Rochester and fled, only to find their way barred by the barons' squires who took clubs to them.

Gradually permission was granted to hold events in England rather than cross the sea to France. At first the contests were still largely mock battles between two teams of mounted knights, sometimes assisted by

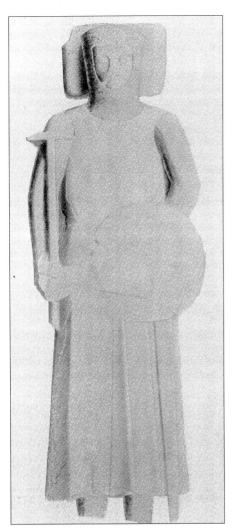

Stothard's drawing of an unusual effigy from Great Malvern Priory, Worcestershire. The pick-axe and circular shield may denote a champion in trial by battle but equally may suggest a man kitted for lighter work on the Welsh borders.

footsoldiers. The area chosen was often a stretch of countryside between two towns or villages and casualties could be heavy. Gradually the arena grew smaller and, by Edward's reign, individual combats between two mounted knights with lances, called jousts, were growing in popularity. At the same time lances were increasingly rebated (blunted) or fitted with a coronel head with prongs instead of a single point, to dissipate the force of a blow in what were known as **jousts of peace**. However, even these remained dangerous contests: in 1268 the heir to the Earl of Warenne died in a tournament at Croydon.

As well as attracting magnates with little to do, tournaments were frequented by younger sons with little prospect of landed wealth, who could use the tournament to win renown and take knights prisoner, when horse and armour or a ransom was paid as forfeit; William Marshal made his fortune by doing the circuit in this way. Moreover the tournament was a useful area for richer men to recruit landless younger sons to their followings. Profit was bound up with honour, and in 1252 both were seen when the Earl of Gloucester had to travel abroad to win these back, since his brother William had lost horses and armour. Notions of chivalry also attached themselves to the tournament, with re-enactments of Arthurian scenes or other stories.

Less formal meetings were called **behourds** and seem to have been staged with the participants wearing linen armour, as happened at Blyth in 1258, the first contest attended by Prince Edward. Even so, deaths occurred at this event and Roger Bigod was brain damaged. There were also still problems with unrest. In 1288 squires dressed as friars and canons pretended to hold a behourd at Boston in Lincolnshire and ended up burning half the town down.

Another social gathering was the **Round Table**, first mentioned in 1228 as a prohibited event and based on the stories of King Arthur. Jousting with blunted weapons and feasting were features of these occasions. At a contest at Walden in 1252 a death was considered an accident until the lance head used was found to be sharp instead of rebated; the knight responsible had had his leg broken by the dead man at a previous tournament. The first English king to hold a Round Table was Edward I in 1284, though this took place at Nefyn in Wales, to celebrate his victories there. Unlike his father, Edward enjoyed participating in tournaments and a number were held until the costs of real wars in Gascony, Wales and Scotland curtailed them. However, the kings now realised their popularity could be boosted by patronising such events. In 1260 Edward took a large company of knights overseas to tournaments, only to be beaten, as he was again two years later.

Crusade

Throughout the 13th century some knights chose to venture on crusade to the Holy Land. The impetus for English knights to take part had come with Richard I as one of the leaders of the Third Crusade in 1190. After his death the monarchy remained influential as to who should be

BELOW **The head of the late 13th century effigy attributed to William Marshal the Younger in the Temple Church, London. The latter has his ventail buckled or perhaps hooked at the side, and what appears to be a fillet of precious metal around the coif. The legs of this figure have poleyns with a lace on the lower edge. Beyond can just be seen the mid-century effigy attributed to his father, William Marshal the Elder.**

allowed to go, though the nobles now were effectively in control of the crusading forces who left the country. For the Fifth Crusade (1218–21) a number of English magnates and barons went overseas, including Ranulf Earl of Chester, Saher de Quincy Earl of Winchester, and Robert FitzWalter. Some, under the leadership of Simon de Montfort, father of that Simon who would make his name in England, joined the crusades against the Albigensian heretics. After the Holy Land was lost in 1291, campaigns against the Moors in Spain or the Teutonic Knights' crusades in Eastern Europe were alternatives.

A crusading background was good for family values. It was a surer way to heaven, since a crusader dying in battle did not have to wait in purgatory, and his lands were expected to be safe while he was away.

Both crusades and tournaments probably assisted in making the knightly class increasingly exclusive.

CAMPAIGNING

Preparations
Mustered troops could be ordered and drilled up to a point, a fact not lost on Simon de Montfort who noted how well the enemy advanced at Evesham in 1265. However, many magnates had little experience of real hostilities and when the Welsh wars broke out it was men such as Otto de Grandison and Hugh de Turberville with fighting experience in France who found themselves favoured by the king. Like Turberville, Luke de Tany had been Seneschal of Gascony and, despite a poor record, was given his own command in 1282 because of his previous position.

Edward needed to co-ordinate the army, since there were many inexperienced commanders, but he never brigaded horse and foot together. Transportation, training for foot and combining arms, the use of the fleet of the Cinque Ports, were all areas of concern. Sheriffs collected food and war material from the counties and from Scotland, Ireland and Gascony. The crown bought at cost price. Some was presumably deducted from the cavalryman's 1 shilling or the footman's 2d for food. Mobilisation could be swift. When the Welsh revolt broke out on 22 March 1282, Edward had the first troops on the payroll by 7 April and the feudal muster ordered for 2 August.

The dismembered body of Simon de Montfort is graphically portrayed in this manuscript illustration. Following the battle of Evesham in 1265, his corpse was treated ignominiously by the royalists. (By permission of the British Library, MS Cotton Nero D II, f.177)

Strategy and tactics

Campaigning could be difficult. John made an abortive attempt to invade Wales in 1211 that failed because of a lack of supplies; Llywelyn and the Welsh collected their belongings and cattle and withdrew into the mountains. In 1265 Simon de Montfort's troops were unable to get their normal food and suffered from having to live off the land in Wales. Edward I fought no major battles in Wales – the ground was wrong for cavalry and the Welsh fought more as guerrillas. Knights were often hampered by the mountainous terrain but the English were nevertheless victorious in two engagements. Edward instead used attrition. He launched his first campaign against Wales both by land and sea, using labourers and woodcutters to make a road through the forests, building castles and cutting off the grain supply from Anglesey. In 1282 a bridge of boats was built to cross to Anglesey.

The king used similar tactics against the Scots. The first campaign in 1296 was completed in just over five months, with Scotland annexed to England. After his victory at Falkirk in 1298 he was able to provision his garrisons. He was in Scotland again in 1300, besieging Caerlaverock castle and leading his armies across the country, but the Scots withdrew and refused battle. English armies would always be hampered by problems of supply in Scotland; the further they ventured, the longer the lifeline to England became. Moreover, many English-held castles were scattered and remote, making it difficult to march swiftly from one to another, or to relieve a fortress if besieged.

Scouts were used to locate enemy forces, after which, the commanders tried to work out the best way to proceed. Armies made use of terrain where possible, and were careful to protect a flank if feasible. William Marshal, in a speech to his troops before the second

BELOW **The effigy of a knight forester in Pershore Abbey, Worcestershire, c.1270–80. The mail hood is open at the throat, the ventail hanging on the left side.**

battle of Lincoln in 1217, pointed out how the enemy's division of his force meant that Marshal could lead all his men against one part alone. Other commanders were less prudent or simply hotheaded. The decision by the Earl of Surrey in 1287 to cross Stirling Bridge with the Scots in near proximity was foolhardy, since there was a wide ford two miles upstream that would have allowed a flank attack, and indeed Sir Richard Lundy had suggested this move. As it turned out, William Wallace and Andrew Murray attacked before even half the English force was across the bridge and the majority of those caught on the wrong bank were crushed.

When Edward was in direct control he proved a good tactician, as he showed at Evesham in 1265. He advanced to stop Simon reaching Kenilworth, and divided his army into three battles to block his escape. Caught in a loop of the River Avon, Simon's vain hope of killing Edward was dashed when the second battle swung into his flank while the third blocked any escape back south.

In his Scottish campaign of 1298, Edward brought 2,500 heavy cavalry and probably about 15,000 infantry. At Falkirk he faced the Scots arrayed in their schiltrons, tightly packed formations presenting a hedge of spears towards any attacker. They may have additionally fortified the position with wooden stakes. Again, disagreement was found among the division leaders: having skirted to the right of wet ground, the Bishop of Durham sensibly wanted to wait for the earls of the left-hand division to come level, and for the king who was bringing up the centre. But the impetuous young Ralph Bassett urged the cavalry on. Swinging out round the flanks, the two English divisions rode down the Scottish archers stationed between the schiltrons, and the Scottish cavalry broke and fled. However, the horsemen could not break the determined Scottish ranks of spears and it was the move by the king to bring up his archers and crossbowmen that helped prevent his knights dashing themselves to pieces. English cavalry deterred the Scots from breaking their ranks, and they were then forced to stand their ground until the archers withdrew, allowing the cavalry finally to break through. Even so, over 100 horses were killed. It should be noted that there appear to have been more cavalrymen in the battle than archers, and that crossbowmen were also used. Edward does not seem as yet to have developed his tactic

Detail showing the strapped cuirass worn under the surcoat but over the mail.

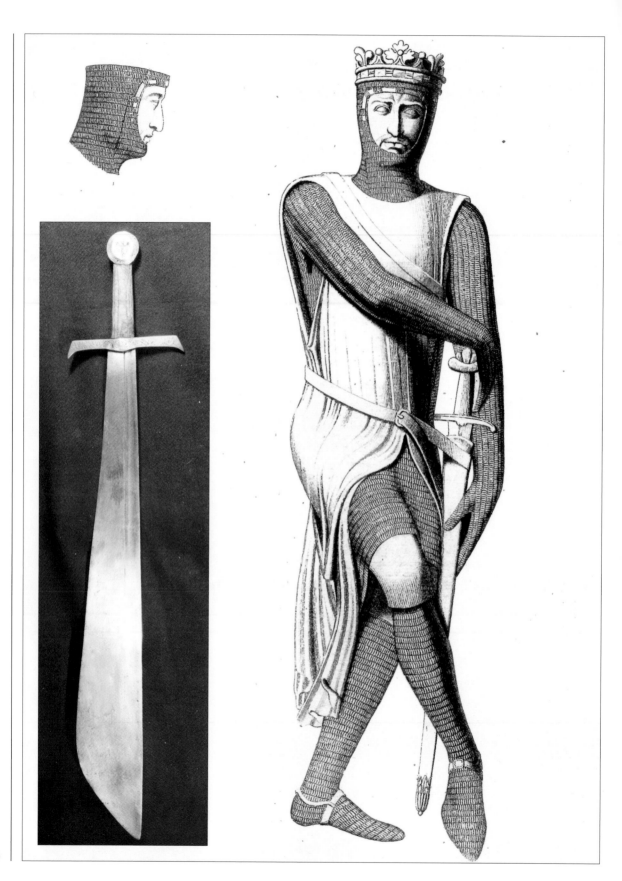

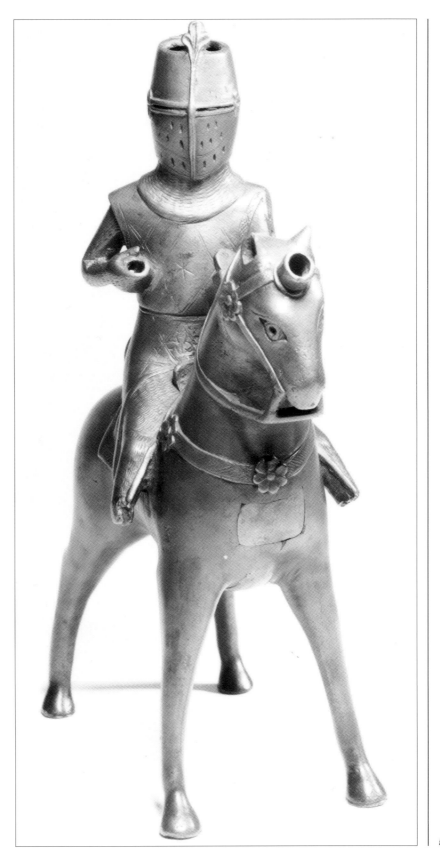

LEFT **The late 13th-century wooden effigy of Robert of Gloucester in Gloucester Cathedral, after Stothard. The surcoat was painted red. His knees are protected additionally by poleyns.**

LEFT INSET **The 13th-century Conyers falchion. (Reproduced by permission of the Dean and Chapter of Durham)**

RIGHT **A late 13th-century copper-alloy aquamanile, designed to carry water, found in the River Tyne near Hexham. It is cast in the shape of a mounted knight, filled via the helm and emptied through a spout on the horse's head. The knight is dressed in a surcoat, but his shield and couched lance are missing, as is the hinged lid, which formed the top of his helm. Rosettes decorate the bridle and breast-band of his mount. (Reproduced by courtesy of the Trustees of the British Museum, Dept of Medieval and Modern Europe, 53, 3–15, 1)**

of using massed longbows to decimate enemy ranks.

Knights at this time still often fought from horseback, changing to their destriers or coursers from the palfreys they used for riding. There is no evidence that cavalry routinely dismounted during the Welsh wars. The charge began as a walk, increasing speed when within suitable range so that the horses would not be blown or the formation disorganised when the final push came. The mounted charge could still be highly effective, the knights riding almost knee to knee with lowered lances in the hope of steam-rolling over the opposition. The lance usually shattered during the first charge, the stump being dropped and, if need be, the sword was drawn, or perhaps a mace or horseman's axe. Inventories show that horses killed in battle largely belong to knights and those with mounts of quality; in other words, the knights formed the front line.

As is obvious from manuscript illustrations, armour was not proof against all weapons: great sheering blows, especially those delivered with a weapon using both hands, could cut through mail and cause horrific injuries. The helms worn, though not particularly heavy, soon grew hot, muffled hearing and limited vision. Men looked to their lord's banner, which was usually carried furled and only broken out when fighting was expected. Its symbolism was of high import; if it fell or was captured there was a risk of panic, and it would be protected by several tough men. Signals were given by trumpet or by hand, especially if the noise made shouting ineffective. Trumpets were also used to call the troops to arms before battle. War cries were used to frighten the enemy and bolster courage.

Another problem with a mounted charge was discipline. As happened at Lewes, the charge by Prince Edward's cavalry was successful but the elated horsemen kept going, pursuing their opponents so far as to put themselves out of the battle as well. The threat of the front line being completely penetrated was one reason commanders sometimes used a reserve, as did Simon de Montfort at Lewes.

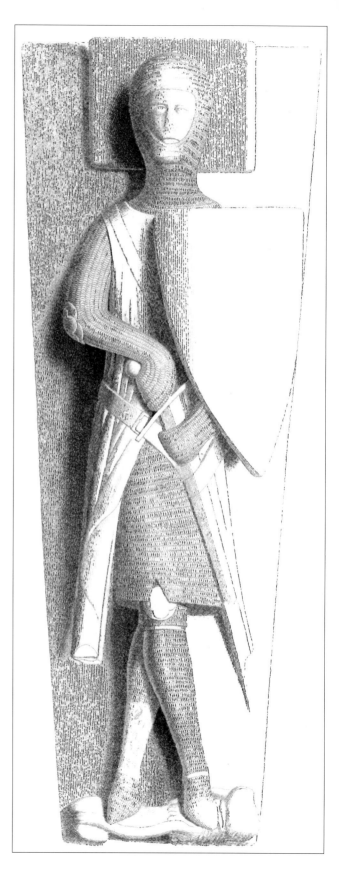

The knights who burst through might turn and strike the rear of the enemy line. The reserve was also quite often the position of the commander, with subordinates controlling the forward battles.

Sieges were more prevalent than set-piece battles. There was less worry of losing all in a single engagement, though a protracted siege was expensive and it became increasingly difficult to hold troops together. Great keeps, or donjons, were by their size difficult to take, as King John found at Rochester in 1215 when he arrived to confront the rebel barons. Having undermined a corner of the donjon, his men found the defenders still resisted for a time from behind the cross-wall inside. The siege lasted almost two months.

By the end of the century castles had perhaps reached their peak of development, as witness the imposing constructions of Edward I in Wales. Several of these, such as Harlech and Beaumaris, were of concentric form, with an inner and outer wall supporting one another all round, and with every defensive trick, such as arrow loops, overhanging wooden hoardings to command the base of the wall, and projecting mural towers to enfilade the wall and effectively cut it into separate sections that could be closed off if gained by an enemy.

But castles were not just for defence, they were bases for mounted knights who could ride out perhaps ten miles and back in a day, or as temporary bases for royal troops to operate against rebels, or vice versa. Edward's Welsh strongholds were as much instruments of conquest as

LEFT **The late 13th-century effigy of William Longespée the Younger, in Salisbury Cathedral. Here is shown a rare instance of additional decorated cups on the elbows, as well as similar poleyns directly attached over the mail at the knees. His sword is an early example of a blade of flattened diamond section. Insulted for his prudence at Mansourah in 1250, William charged into a certain trap and, having lost his left foot, right arm and left hand, was hacked to pieces where he fell.**

BELOW **Detail of the elbow defence.**

defended bases. Similarly castles provided fortified resting places for field forces, and their garrisons could be used to enlarge such a force. Harrying the lands of one's enemy was sometimes a prelude to a siege, and was a way to deny food, kill peasants and so his economy, and insult his lordship.

Sieges could be costly and involve much organisation, sometimes drawing craftsmen from all over England, as that of Bedford by Henry III in 1224 shows. The king summoned much of the kingdom's resources, with carpenters, miners, stone-cutters and quarriers brought to the scene together with all sorts of equipment, such as timber, ropes and tallow for siege engines. We also glimpse the necessary luxuries of the lords: as well as his armour, King Henry's tents were sent by cart from London, together with comforts such as wine, pepper, almonds, cinnamon, saffron and ginger.

Yet the real business was dangerous. Lord Richard de Argentan was hit in the stomach by a crossbow bolt that went through his armour, and six other knights were killed. It took four assaults, each time advancing further into the castle, before the defenders yielded. Quarter was usually given if a place surrendered but was in the gift of the besiegers if a castle were taken by force. At Bedford the garrison had already been excommunicated by the Archbishop of Canterbury and King Henry, angry at the resistance he had met in a siege lasting eight weeks, hung William de Bréauté outside the gates with his knights. As a note of leniency he did, however, allow them to be absolved of their excommunication. At Rochester, too, John seems to have wanted to

The late 13th-century effigy of a knight in the Temple Church, London, sometimes attributed to Gilbert Marshal. A strapped cuirass is just visible in the gap in the surcoat under the armpit. Note the shields and bars decorating the guige.

hang the garrison, until it was pointed out that this might prompt other rebels to do the same to royal garrisons.

Perhaps the most celebrated siege in 13th-century England was that of Kenilworth in 1266, when supporters of Simon de Montfort took refuge there after their leader's death at Evesham. The siege by Henry III and the Lord Edward lasted six months and only ended on terms of surrender. Mining was impossible because of the wide water defences. As well as using siege towers and catapults, several attacks were launched by knights on the siege lines causing much damage and loss of life. This was one reason knights were important to the defence of a castle. Yet food was equally important, and lack of provisions was a major reason the defenders asked for a truce, saying that if no help came in 40 days, they would surrender. They were then allowed to march out with full military honours.

Siege warfare also demonstrated, as at Bedford, that knights could fight effectively on foot, since a mounted man was not much use against a wall unless a gate was forced. Conversely he was needed in siege towers or on scaling ladders, or as a strong pair of hands, as at Dover in 1216 when the French Prince Louis mined a gate tower, only to find the breach blocked by timbers hastily inserted by Hubert de Burgh and his men.

Knights could have long military careers. William Marshal was 70 at the battle of Lincoln in 1217. Some, however, did not like the idea of campaigning. Knights knew the fear of death in combat but they were trained to fight and knew it was their duty to do so. They might hope that their enemies would wish to capture rather than kill them, since their ransom was a tempting tool of moderation. Certainly in some battles few knights were killed and this can only partly be ascribed to better armour. There was also the desire to capture knights for themselves (in war or tournament), or for plunder. Valour and loyalty might be rewarded by the lord or by the king, in the form of wealth or forfeited lands.

BIBLIOGRAPHY

Barber, Richard, *The Knight and Chivalry*, Longman Group Ltd., London, 1970.

Barber, Richard, and Barker, Juliet, *Tournaments: Jousts Chivalry and Pageants in the Middle Ages*, The Boydell Press, Woodbridge, 1989.

View of the head of the Temple effigy, showing the lace of the ventail and what appears to be a fillet around the head.

Blair, Claude, *European Armour*, B. T. Batsford Ltd., London, 1958.

Bradbury, J., *The Medieval Archer*, The Boydell Press, Woodbridge, 1985.

Bradbury, J., *The Medieval Siege*, The Boydell Press, Woodbridge, 1992.

Burgess, M., *The Mail-Maker's Technique*, London, 1953.

Contamine, Philippe (trans Jones, Michael), *War in the Middle Ages*, Basil Blackwell, Oxford, 1984.

Coss, Peter, *The Knight in Medieval England 1000–1400*, Alan Sutton Publishing Ltd., Stroud, 1993.

Cunnington, C. Willet and Phillis, *Handbook of English Mediaeval Costume*, Faber and Faber Ltd., London, 1969.

Davis, R. H. C., *The Medieval Warhorse*, Thames and Hudson Ltd., London, 1989.

Dufty, R., and Read, W., *European Armour*, HMSO, London, 1968.

Edge, David, and Paddock, John Miles, *Arms and Armour of the Medieval Knight*, Bison Books, London, 1988.

Foss, Michael, *Chivalry*, Michael Jospeh Ltd., London, 1975.

Gies, Frances, *The Knight in History*, Robert Hale Ltd., London, 1986.

Keen, Maurice, *Chivalry*, Yale University Press, London, 1984.

Koch, H. W., *Medieval Warfare*, Bison Books Ltd., London, 1978.

Mann, Sir James, *Wallace Collection Catalogues. European Arms and Armour*, 2 vols., The Trustees of the Wallace Collection, London, 1962.

Norman, A.V.B., *Wallace Collection Catalogues. European Arms and Armour Supplement*, The Trustees of the Wallace Collection, London, 1986.

Morris, J. E., *The Welsh Wars of Edward I*, OUP, Oxford, 1901

Oakeshott, R. Ewart, *The Sword in the Age of Chivalry*, Lutterworth Press, London, 1964.

Pfaffenbichler, M., *Armourers*, British Museum Press, London, 1992.

Prestwich, M., *Armies and Warfare in the Middle Ages*, York University Press, London, 1996.

Rudorff, Raymond, *The Knights and their World*, Cassell and Company Ltd., London, 1974.

Stenton, Doris, *English Society in the Early Middle Ages*, The Pelican History of England 3, Penguin Books Ltd., Harmondsworth, 1965.

Thompson, M. W., *The Rise of the Castle*, CUP, Cambridge, 1991.

Turnbull, Stephen, *The Book of the Medieval Knight*, London, 1985.

Verbruggen, J. F., *The Art of Warfare in Western Europe during the Middle Ages*, The Boydell Press, Woodbridge, 1997.

Walden, Howard de, *Some Feudal Lords and their Seals* (1903), Crécy Books, Clifton, 1984.

GLOSSARY

Aketon A padded coat, usually quilted vertically, which was worn beneath mail to absorb blows, or on its own by ordinary soldiers.

Ailette A small board of wood or parchment worn at the shoulder and usually painted with heraldic arms.

Arçons The *bow* and *cantle* of a saddle.

Arming cap A padded and quilted cap worn under the mail *coif*, and sometimes over it to support a helm.

Backplate Plate armour for the back.

Baleyn Whalebone. The naem refers to the baleen plates in the mouths of some species, which act as filters.

Bard Armoured covering for a horse.

Basinet At this date a small open-faced helmet.

Baudekin A silk cloth with a warp of gold thread.

Bec-de-faucon A staff weapon consisting of an axe- or hammer-head backed by a beak like that of a falcon.

Behourd A less formal version of the Tournament

The late 13th-century effigy of Edmund Crouchback, Earl of Lancaster (died 1296), in Westminster Abbey. He wears poleyns on his knees. The circlet probably secures a cervellière beneath the mail hood, which appears to be separate. A lace at the wrist prevents the mail dragging. (Copyright: 'Dean and Chapter of Westminster')

57

Bill A staff weapon derived from a hedging bill, consisting of a broad convex hooked blade with a spike at the top and rear.

Bodkin A long arrow-head without barbs, for piercing armour, especially mail.

Bow The front of the saddle.

Braies Loose linen drawers tied with a running string.

Brases Carrying straps fitted inside a shield.

Breastplate Plate armour for the chest and stomach.

Breaths Holes in a helmet for ventilation and increased vision.

Broad-head A wide barbed arrow-head with long cutting edges, used for hunting or maiming war-horses.

Burnet A brown cloth.

Buskins Leather boots.

Byssine A fine cotton or flax material.

Cantle The rear part of a saddle.

Cap-à-pie Fully armed, literally 'head to foot'.

Caparison Cloth, or occasionally mail, covering or housing for a horse, the former often used to carry the owner's coat of arms.

Cervellière A small hemispherical steel skull-cap.

Chape A metal terminal fitted over the tip of a scabbard to protect it.

Chappe A small leather rain-guard fitted over the sword cross to protect the blade in the scabbard.

Chausses Stockings, either of cloth or mail.

Coat of plates Body armour consisting of a canvas jacket inside which plates are riveted. The outside is usually faced with cloth or leather. Also called 'pair of plates', 'hauberk of plates', 'cote à plates' or 'plates'.

Coif A mail hood. Also a cloth cap secured under the chin with ties. See also *Arming cap*.

Conroi A unit of cavalry, often in multiples of ten

Constabularia A unit of men, probably ten.

Coronel A small crown of points used instead of a single sharp head on lances for *jousts of peace*. Several points spread the impact of the blow.

Cote The tunic.

Courser A war-horse.

Couter Plate defence for the elbow.

Cuirass Armour for the torso, usually denoting the breast- and back-plates.

Cuir-bouilli Hardened leather that has been boiled or soaked before shaping.

Cuirie Solid body armour, presumably of leather, sometimes reinforced by circular plates.

Destrier The largest, strongest and most expensive war-horse.

Dubbing The tap on the shoulder with a sword to make a new knight.

Enarmes See *Brases*.

Falchion A cleaver-like single-edged short sword.

Fitchet A vertical slit made in *super-tunics* with no side opening, allowing access to keys or purse hung from the tunic girdle.

Gambeson A padded coat usually quilted vertically. The term generally refers to a coat worn over the armour rather than beneath it.

Gamboised cuisse A padded and quilted tubular thigh defence, sometimes richly decorated.

Garde-corps Long garment with wide tubular sleeves provided with slits for the arms to pass through.

Garnache A beltless garment cut like the *tabard* but with shoulder line wide enough to cover the elbows.

Gauntlet Defence for the hand and wrist.

Gisarme Also called *guisarme*. A staff weapon consisting of a convex axe-head with the lowest point attached to the shaft.

Glaive A staff weapon with a long convex cutting edge.

Gorget A plate collar to guard the throat.

Graper A metal or leather band nailed round the lance behind the grip.

Greave Plate armour for the lower leg.

Guard-chain A chain that, from the end of the century, was sometimes attached to the waist belt and fixed by a toggle to the helm, sword or dagger to prevent loss.

Guige The carrying strap of a shield.

Guisarme See *Gisarme*.

Hackney A riding horse.

Hauberk A mail coat.

Haubergeon A shorter version of the *hauberk*.

Helm A large helmet enclosing the entire head.

Herald An official employed by a king or nobleman, and who wore his arms. Heralds delivered messages and identified coats-of-arms.

Herygoud See *Garde-corps*.

Hure A cap.

Jamber Defence for the lower leg.

Jousts of peace Contest between two mounted opponents using blunted lances.

Jousts of war Contest between two mounted opponents using sharp lances.

Kettle-hat Open-faced helmet with a broad brim.

King-of-arms The rank above that of herald.

Lame A strip or plate of steel, sometimes used to provide articulation in armour.

Lance A long spear used on horseback.

Lists The tournament arena where combats took place.

Locket A metal mount to protect the mouth of a scabbard or sheath.

Mail Armour made from interlinked iron rings. Most were riveted but sometimes alternate lines of riveted and welded rings were used.

Muffler A mail mitten.

Nasal The noseguard on a helmet.

Palfrey A good riding horse.

Pelisson A *super-tunic* lined with fur.

Pike A long spear used by infantry.

Poleyn Solid armour for the knee.

Pourpoint See *Aketon*.

Pursuivant The rank below that of herald, identified by wearing the *tabard* sideways.

Rebated point A weapon point that has been blunted, for use in tournament contests.

Rouncy A horse suitable only for casual; riding

Scale Armour made from overlapping scales secured to a backing.

Schynbald A solid plate shin defense.

Shaffron Plate defence for a horse's head.

Siclaton See *Baudekin*.

Skull The main part of a helmet covering the top and sides of the head above the ears. Also a simple metal cap.

Spaudler A plate shoulder-defence.

Sumpter A pack horse or mule.

Super-tunic A garment worn over the tunic. Also called a *surcoat*.

Surcoat In military parlance, a cloth garment worn over armour, usually lined and mostly sleeveless. In civilian parlance, a *super-tunic*, sometimes similar to the military version.

Tabard A sleeveless *super-tunic* stitched or clasped together at waist level.

Tang The continuation of a sword blade that passes through the hilt.

Tournament Originally a contest between two teams but later used to embrace the developed form in which jousting and foot combat also took place.

Tourney A term used to denote the mounted team event during a tournament, to distinguish it from other events.

Trapper See *Caparison*.

Ventail Flap of mail worn across the chin and sometimes also covering the mouth.

Wambais See *Aketon*.

COLOUR PLATE COMMENTARY

A: KNIGHT C.1210

1 The central figure wears a mail coat as a main body defence. It reaches the knees, while the arms extend to form mail mittens. Beneath can be seen a vertically quilted **aketon**. The **surcoat** is here without a waist belt. At the beginning of the century, and increasingly rarely thereafter, some shields were still fitted with a metal domed boss, secured by rivets through a flange. This was a relic from the days of circular shields, when a hole was cut out of the board to accommodate the hand grasping the grip, and the boss covered it. Circular infantry bucklers continued to use a central grip.

2 **Mail** coat worn without covering and lacking mittens.

3 Mail **mufflers** or mittens. To aid grip, the palm of the hand is covered by leather or a glove stitched inside; a slit allows the hand to protrude. A thong threaded through the links at the wrist prevents them bunching over the hand.

4 Interlinked riveted mail rings.

5 Iron scale armour.

6 Helmet fitted with face mask.

7 Rounded style of helmet that would supersede the conical form in popularity, here with a **nasal**.

8 Cylindrical style, here with a nasal; it occasionally tapered gently to the brim and was sometimes drawn up to a very slight apex. The top section is secured by overlapping the side and riveting all around.

9 The controversial chin defence.

10 Conical helmet with conjectural padded lining, scalloped at the top and with drawer string.

11 Mail coif thrown back to show padded **arming cap** and lined **aventail**, and with the latter laced in place.

12 Strip of mail to guard leg.

13 Mail **chausses** over hose, and tied to waist belt.

14 Iron prick spur; the leather is bolted to the terminal *c.*1200–1300.

15 **Surcoat** worn as a super-tunic.

16 Long tunic with magyar sleeves; cross-gartering sometimes worn by the rich at this date. Stalked hat.

17 Sword, *c.* 1200 or earlier.

18 Sword, *c.* 1200–1300.

19 Sword, *c.* 1200–1300.

20 Exploded view of sword hilt to show wooden two-part grip.

21 Mace with moulded copper-alloy head, *c.*1200.

B: THE HUNT

Hunting provided exercise for knights and squires, as well as the prospect of additional fresh meat. Deer hunting could take two forms. The animals were sometimes hunted from horseback. Later medieval evidence suggests that a single deer was picked out (harboured), then relays of two or three couples of hounds were set along paths the quarry was likely to use. Once the chosen deer and about half the pursuing hounds had passed, the huntsman slipped his own dogs to join the chase and revitalise the others. Knights and ladies rode after them, blowing various notes on their horns to signal to the others what was happening. When the beast was brought to bay, it was usual to wait for the lord to appear, who would draw his sword and dispatch the animal by a thrust through the shoulder into the heart, taking his chances against the antlers. If he was late, huntsmen might finish the stag before it could kill or wound the dogs; sometimes it was first hamstrung from behind to lessen the danger.

The other form of deer hunt was the bow and stable, the line of men who, by noise and gesture, would drive the game towards the waiting bowmen. The huntsmen, armed with bows or crossbows, took up a position preferably along the slopes of a wooded valley, into which the deer were driven by beaters. Wounded or escaping deer could be scented out or seized by the huntsmen's dogs; those avoiding this might be blocked by additional huntsmen with large greyhounds positioned some distance beyond the main group. Wounded animals were liable to drop from their wounds in any case, for the broad swallow-tailed hunting arrowheads had barbs to prevent them from dropping out, and long cutting edges to sever blood vessels.

The wild boar was becoming increasingly rare in England. Having been chased by greyhounds, large muscular dogs called alaunts were used to hold a cornered boar. The huntsman took his life in his hands, since the razor-sharp tusks could disembowel or sever blood vessels. He used a boar spear, a wide-bladed weapon with lugs at the base of the blade in case the enraged animal pushed up the weapon in its effort to reach him.

The other passion of the rich was hunting with hawks and falcons. Some birds were even kept on a perch in a lord's chamber. The most prized were peregrine falcons and gerfalcons, the power dive of the former a sight to behold. Many small mammals and birds caught by the birds of prey found their way to the dinner table.

C: HORSES

Horses were essential to a knight, and included a war-horse, the **destrier** or **courser**, a good riding horse, the **palfrey**, and **rounceys** for squires or servants. **Sumpters** for baggage, or wagon horses, were also needed. Replacements were necessary, too; in 1266, 38 men took 64 horses when they went to garrison Nottingham castle. By the early 13th century prices were rising fast. An average warhorse could cost up to £50, and by the end of the century well over £60 (for barons and bannerets between 60–120 marks). Some lords offered horses to the king in lieu of some other payment. Horses were brought in from foreign areas such as Spain, Lombardy and France, but royal studs were also known. By Edward I's reign they were dotted about the country. Edward also imported horses, especially Spanish stock, to improve the mounts of his cavalry. Knights bachelor rode *equi* of 20–40 marks (£15–£30), while rounceys for squires and sergeants cost £5–£8, or £12–£15 for the best examples, such as for troopers in the king's *familia*. In 1295 the horses of stipendiary troops were valued in case replacement was necessary.

1 The war-horse is shown in a full **caparison**. The tail was often enclosed under the cloth. Solid **shaffrons**

**A 13th or 14th century stirrup, decorated with silver inlay.
(By courtesy of the Trustees of the Armouries, VI.485)**

for the horse's head were certainly in use during the 13th century, but English illustrations are virtually non-existent. This depiction is based on a mid-13th century Spanish manuscript and has been interpreted as *cuir-bouilli*, described in the Windsor Tournament Roll of 1278. A fan crest was occasionally worn. The war saddle has a high **cantle** that curves slightly round the rider's body, while the bow usually curved slightly forward. The long stirrups produced a military riding posture, giving a secure seat but preventing the knight from standing in his stirrups. There were often two girths, and usually a breast-band, sometimes fastened around the cantle for added support. Crupper bands might also be used.

2 A mail **trapper** and chain reins to prevent cutting.
3 Palfrey with harness decorated with pendants and bells.
4 Harness pendant with backplate secured by a rivet at each corner, shown with suggested coloured insert, Museum of London.
5 Snaffle bit.
6 Curb bit, Museum of London.
7 Stirrup.
8 Bridle with snaffle.
9–11 Bridle styles with curb bits, *c.*1250.

D: MAGNA CARTA

The strong government machinery and laws of John's father, Henry II, had kept working after the latter's death in 1189. When John came to the throne in 1199 many barons were tired of the restraints, and the loss of Normandy in 1204 was compounded by the failure of the Anglo-German allies at the battle of Bouvines in 1214. Numbers of English barons met together, partly under cover of tournaments and, having seized London despite a rather poor campaign, representatives came to the king on 10 June where he was camped amongst the water meadows by the River Thames near Staines. Agreements were reached, and on 15 June the armed rebels appeared to meet the king at Runnymede, a small island in the river. Many of the older lords stayed loyal to John, and it was often the younger men who joined the revolt, such as the son of William Marshal, Earl of Pembroke. There was a strong northern faction of lesser barons, who perhaps incited the movement, notable among them Eustace de Vesci (with hand on shield), but the heavier weight was to the south and east. The rebels were led by a roughneck called Robert FitzWalter (who brought a family group with him), here seen pointing at the document with his comrade, Saher de Quency, Earl of Winchester. The seal press stands ready to impress the royal seal on the wax. Having learned the rebel terms, John reluctantly agreed to the Articles of the Barons, which would later be set down as the Magna Carta, or 'Great Charter'. It was actually a document designed to voice the complaints of the barons rather than being set out to benefit the common man as many have since come to believe, though among the many feudal issues it addresses, it does specify that no free man is to be unlawfully imprisoned and no one denied the right of justice. As soon as John felt strong enough he repudiated Magna Carta, and civil war broke out.

E: KNIGHT C.1250

1 The **mail coat** remained the main body defence, but here solid **schynbalds** over the mail **chausses** protect the shins and poleyns guard the knees.
2 Helms, from statues on Wells Cathedral, c.1230–40.
3 The kettle hat had been known from the mid-12th century. It was usually worn by those below the rank of knight, but already in the mid-13th century we hear of King Louis of France exchanging his helm for the lighter kettle hat, which allowed more air to the face, especially useful when crusading. Two forms, shown here, seem to have been used in this period. The skull was made from two or four pieces, the joints covered by applied riveted bands, and the brim riveted on.
4 Shaped **arming cap** for a **helm** worn under the mail **coif**, held in position by a lace through the links.
5 **Arming cap** with padded roll and a solid collar, from Wells, c.1230–40.
6 Buckled padded **ventail**, covered collar, and **cervellière** worn over **arming cap** but under **coif**.
7 Sleeved **surcoat** with dagged edges.
8 **Gamboised cuisse**, which would be tied to a waist belt.
9 **Poleyn** attached to mail.
10 **Poleyn** attached to **gamboised cuisse**.
11 Sword from the Ouse at Ely, Museum of Archaeology, Cambridge, c.1150–1250.
12 Great sword, c.1250–1300.

13 Scabbard detail.
14 Flanged mace.
15 Knobbed mace.
16 Various styles of dagger.
17 Horseman's axe.
18 Long axe.
19 Short glaive.

F: THE BATTLE OF LEWES 14 MAY 1264

The charge of Prince Edward's cavalry routs the Londoners at the battle of Lewes. Not a great deal is known of the deployment of the divisions at this battle. Henry III faced Simon de Montfort outside Lewes, with perhaps 10,000 men in three battles, with Richard of Cornwall commanding one and Prince Edward leading the right-hand division. It seems that Simon had about half that number; he placed Henry de Montfort on his right, Gloucester in the centre and Nicholas de Segrave on his left, while he led the reserve behind Gloucester. The royalists may have had 3,000 cavalry to Simon's 500. Apparently the rebels made small white cloth crosses which were sewn on to their breasts and backs. De Segrave's banner (sable, three garbs argent) is visible on the right. Notice how the Prince's coat-of-arms is reversed on the horse's right side, a common practice to show heraldic animals facing towards the horse's head. Edward's royalists chased the Londoners off the field, and did not return for some time. Simon probably now launched his own attack, which crumpled the royalist centre, Cornwall taking refuge in a windmill. Despite gallant resistance by the king, Simon swung in his reserve. Scattered fighting took place around the river and town, seized by the rebels before Edward returned. The padded aketon worn by the infantryman on the left may be of the same form as that worn under a full mail coat. When collars are shown it is not known if they formed part of the aketon itself, nor whether such collars were of padding or of a solid material as sometimes noted in accounts.

G: MEDICAL SERVICES

The chances of receiving decent attention when wounded depended very much on a knight's status and on luck. The great magnates might have a surgeon, or perhaps could hope the king would lend his own man when on campaign together. Medical men would travel with the army but they were decidedly not for the ordinary soldiers, or indeed for the ordinary knights, there being very few for the entire army. In 1298–1300, during the wars with Scotland, come the first accounts of an organised medical service. The king had his physician with two servants, or juniors; also his surgeon, and another man (like the two servants, ranked as esquire) who was on half the pay of the physician and surgeon. The king's surgeon was his own personal doctor. Such men had trained perhaps at the great schools of Salerno in Southern Italy. Their services were limited and most ordinary soldiers were simply released from service to find help in the nearest town or monastery. Families could also help, depending on the nature of the wound. Knights' wives were often proficient in using salves and in stitching up cuts, having been taught this during their own training as the daughters of knights. However, this depended on either the wives travelling with the army or else the fighting being close enough for the wounded man to be taken home. The royal surgeon wears a long, formal garde-corps, denoting his status. Though herbs and poultices, egg yolks and boiled nettles might be used to soothe wounds, boiling elder oil was for centuries a recognised treatment for open wounds such as this sword cut to the shoulder. The assistant wears a short-sleeved super-tunic and has helpfully but misguidedly prepared a red-hot iron, the standard remedy for sealing bleeding vessels after amputation, after which the skin was pulled tight and stitched. Cautery was also used for most types of wound by the barber-surgeons (who also shaved men) in whose hands ordinary knights might end up.

H: KNIGHT C. 1290

1 By the late 13th century many knights were wearing a **coat of plates**, or occasionally even a **cuirie**, beneath their **surcoat** but over their **mail coat**. This figure of a knight of the Hastings family has substantial poleyns protecting the front and sides of the knee. The **coif** is now separate, and hidden under it he has a whalebone collar. From about 1275 **aillettes** were sometimes worn by knights, being small rectangular or, rarely, diamond-shaped or circular, boards attached to the shoulders and painted with the knight's arms. It used to be thought that aillettes provided protection for the neck but, since some parchment examples are described, it seems they were wholly for display. The **helm** is more pointed, with a chain and toggle to the belt to sling it and help prevent loss in battle. Crests were secured by laces through a ring of holes on the helm, and this join could be disguised by wrapping a cloth around it and allowing it to hang down the back of the helm, where it may have helped give protection from heat. This would become known as the wreath and lambrequin in later heraldic display; at this date it was less fussy. Sometimes the ends of the cloth hang down like a scarf, at other times it appears to be like a single broad rectangle of cloth.

2 **Helm**, Italian, c.1300.

4 Kettle hat.

5 Separate **coif**, with rear slit tightened by a lace, obviating the need for a **ventail**.

6 **Couter**, from effigy of William Longespée the Younger, Salisbury Cathedral.

7 Suggested appearance of a reinforced **surcoat**.

8 **Coat of plates**, showing vertical plates riveted inside.

9 Reconstruction of a gauntlet covered in whalebone plates.

10 Reconstruction of a rowel spur, from fragments, c.1300, Museum of London. The ornamental swan may allude to the Swan Knight legend with which some families associated. The decorated spur arm was worn on the outside of the foot.

11 Sword belt secured to scabbard by two laces, from late 13th-century effigy of Gilbert Marshal, Temple Church, London.

12 Great sword, Burrell Collection, Glasgow, c.1270–1330.

13 Sword, c.1250–1350.

14 Sword, Royal Armouries, c.1250–80.

15 **Garnache** with hood.

RIGHT **Stothard's drawing of the effigy of a de Vere in the Church of St Mary, Hatfield Broad Oak, Essex. The figure has a separate coif and gamboised cuisses with small poleyns attached. Its date is debatable but may be c.1300.**

INDEX

Figures in **bold** refer to illustrations

COMPANION SERIES FROM OSPREY

ESSENTIAL HISTORIES
Concise studies of the motives, methods and repercussions of human conflict, spanning history from ancient times to the present day. Each volume studies one major war or arena of war, providing an indispensable guide to the fighting itself, the people involved, and its lasting impact on the world around it.

MEN-AT-ARMS
The uniforms, equipment, insignia, history and organisation of the world's military forces from earliest times to the present day. Authoritative text and full-colour artwork, photographs and diagrams bring over 5,000 years of history vividly to life.

ELITE
This series focuses on uniforms, equipment, insignia and unit histories in the same way as Men-at-Arms but in more extended treatments of larger subjects, also including personalities and techniques of warfare.

NEW VANGUARD
The design, development, operation and history of the machinery of warfare through the ages. Photographs, full-colour artwork and cutaway drawings support detailed examinations of the most significant mechanical innovations in the history of human conflict.

ORDER OF BATTLE
The greatest battles in history, featuring unit-by-unit examinations of the troops and their movements as well as analysis of the commanders' original objectives and actual achievements. Colour maps including a large fold-out base map, organisational diagrams and photographs help the reader to trace the course of the fighting in unprecedented detail.

CAMPAIGN
Accounts of history's greatest conflicts, detailing the command strategies, tactics, movements and actions of the opposing forces throughout the crucial stages of each campaign. Full-colour battle scenes, 3-dimensional 'bird's-eye views', photographs and battle maps guide the reader through each engagement from its origins to its conclusion.

AIRCRAFT OF THE ACES
Portraits of the elite pilots of the 20th century's major air campaigns, including unique interviews with surviving aces. Unit listings, scale plans and full-colour artwork combine with the best archival photography available to provide a detailed insight into the experience of war in the air.

COMBAT AIRCRAFT
The world's greatest military aircraft and combat units and their crews, examined in detail. Each exploration of the leading technology, men and machines of aviation history is supported by unit listings and other data, artwork, scale plans, and archival photography.